# CARING FOR THE CARERS

THE CARE SERIES

# Caring
# for the
# Carers

**CHRISTINE LEDGER**

SERIES EDITOR
REVD DR NIGEL M DE S CAMERON

KINGSWAY PUBLICATIONS
EASTBOURNE

Unless otherwise indicated, biblical quotations are from
the Holy Bible: New International Version, copyright ©
International Bible Society 1973, 1978, 1984. Anglicisation ©
Hodder & Stoughton 1984

RSV = Revised Standard Version
copyrighted 1946, 1952, © 1971, 1973 by the
Division of Education and Ministry of the
National Council of the Churches of Christ in the USA

*Front cover photo: The Image Bank*

**British Library Cataloguing in Publication Data**

Ledger, Chris
Caring for the carers.
I. Title
649.8

ISBN 0 86065 967 4

Printed in Great Britain for
KINGSWAY PUBLICATIONS LTD
1 St Anne's Road, Eastbourne, E Sussex BN21 3UN by
Clays Ltd. St. Ives plc
Typeset by J&L Composition Ltd, Filey, North Yorkshire

# Contents

PART 3: USEFUL INFORMATION

# Introduction to the Series

All around us, Christians are waking up to their responsibility to *care* – for one another, and for all their neighbours in God's world. The old 'social gospel' has been discredited. It tried to rewrite the message and mission of the church as a social and political programme. Many evangelical Christians responded by retreating into a pietism which denied, in effect, that the gospel had social and political implications at all. But more and more they are being called back to their historic role as the heirs of Wilberforce and Shaftesbury. With a fresh confidence in its biblical mandate, the evangelical conscience has reawakened from its fearful slumbers.

Around twenty years ago, two historic developments marked the beginnings of this decisive move towards the recovery of our evangelical heritage. One was the establishment by the Evangelical Alliance of TEAR Fund, to channel evangelical care to needy people overseas. The other was the setting up of the nationwide Festival of Light – now known as CARE (Christian Action, Research and Education) – to channel evangelical concern for the nation. CARE expressed Christian concern through both practical caring initiatives and public, political campaigning.

The roots of CARE's understanding of its mission lie in our stewardship of God's world (which stems from our creation) and our obligations of neighbour-love (underlined anew in Jesus Christ). We have no option but to care for others; and there are two ways in which we may do so – by practical caring for those round about us, and by campaigning for the defence and enhancement of the Christian values of the nation.

This *CARE series* spans these twin concerns. Some books address major public questions, which may be highly controversial. Others focus on practical issues of Christian caring. We pray that this series will help many Christians think through our obligation to be 'salt and light' in society, as loving neighbours and responsible stewards.

NIGEL M DE S CAMERON

# Foreword

Some years ago, when I was Vicar of a busy parish, my wife and I had to look after an elderly relative. Eileen tells the tale in this book. Looking back now on that very tough period we only wish we had the resources of Christine Ledger's book to guide us! Indeed, this is central to the first thing I want to say – I really cannot think of any other Christian book which addresses the subject of 'caring for the carers' and, furthermore, it does not give advice from afar off but is a practical, down-to-earth resource rooted in a firm Christian conviction that God loves and cares for us.

There is another sound reason why I felt honoured to write this Foreword. Mrs Christine Ledger has been a personal friend for many years, and I therefore know that this excellent book is not written by an idealistic 'do-gooder' but by a professional Christian lady who is a trained counsellor as well as a caring person.

This, then, is a book that ought to be on every minister's shelves and, I would suggest, in the home of any person who might one day find herself or himself at the point when caring passes into that area when they feel alone and forgotten.

+George Cantuar
Archbishop of Canterbury

# Acknowledgements

I wish to express my appreciation to all those who made this book possible, particularly Eileen Carey, Steve Hepden, Julia Madgwick, Jean Tame and David Taylor who have so openly and sensitively shared their experiences as carers. I am grateful to Chris Orme, without whose encouragement and constructive help this book would never have found its way into print; for Sylvia Mason whose professional help I valued; for Sarah Birchall who spent many an evening on the word processor; and for the other typists, particularly Sylvia Robson. Finally, how can I express adequately my appreciation to my husband, John, and daughters, Julia and Fiona, for all their support and encouragement.

# 1

## *The Carers*

Ann, recently widowed and in her early sixties, has a full-time job. She is not paid for it or even thanked for it, yet she does it willingly, uncomplainingly and unceasingly. She never has a day off and rarely an unbroken night. Ann, an only child, looks after her ninety-year-old mother who is bedridden and confused and cannot be left for long. Ann is trapped in her own house. She does not drive, and her own hearing problems make it difficult for her to use the telephone, which increases her sense of isolation. She belongs to a lively, caring fellowship, yet she can only depend on a few hours' freedom once a week. Ann is a typical carer in our society; although she doesn't complain, she feels forgotten.

In recent years the word 'carer' has come to mean anybody other than a paid worker who is looking after disabled, ill or elderly relatives or friends who cannot manage at home without help. Carers are ordinary people: the parents of a child with a mental handicap, a husband whose wife has senile dementia, or a daughter looking after her terminally ill mother.

Six million people in Great Britain have caring responsibilities, and 1·7 million have a dependent person living in the same household. Most carers are aged between forty and sixty, and six out of ten are women. Carers come from all educational backgrounds and social groups. Their circumstances vary enormously. Ann, for example, doesn't have a washing machine, yet she looks after an incontinent mother.

Other factors affecting carers include their economic position, the severity of the condition of the person cared for, and the overall support and help available (which depends upon the location of the person cared for). The mother of a handicapped child said:

> I feel I am in a prison – I can rarely get away from the physical and emotional demands of caring for my son who has special needs.

Caring is time-consuming work – twenty per cent of carers devote at least twenty hours a week to the care of their dependant, and if they live in the same household a greater commitment of at least fifty hours a week is common (with fifty-nine per cent of carers over sixty-five giving this amount of time). It is not surprising that as many as sixty per cent of these carers themselves at some time suffer physical or mental illness caused by the relentless strain of being a carer.

The quality of carers' own lives diminishes as they often have to give up salaried jobs, and their social life can be severely restricted. Hobbies, recreation and friends must all take second place to the job of caring; a job which may last for years on end with no training given.

Carers find themselves looking after dependants

for many different reasons – out of love, from a sense of duty, or perhaps because they feel they have no choice. For some, taking this responsibility is relatively easy; for others, it becomes increasingly difficult. Carers usually put their own needs second – or ignore them altogether. It can appear selfish to think about oneself when the dependant's needs appear so much greater. But carers *do* have needs.

## A manifesto for carers

Carers need:

Recognition of their contribution

Recognition of their own needs as individuals in their own right

Opportunities for a break (for short and longer times)

Practical help to lighten the physical burden of caring

Someone to talk to about their own emotional needs

Information about available support groups.

So what do we need to *know, understand* and *be able to do* in order to care for the carers? Exactly *which* insights, strategies, resources, perspectives and courses of action will ease the carer's burden? As much as possible within the limits of the printed page, this CARE series book serves as a help and guide to answer these questions. My aim has been not just to provide an information handbook –

though the book does offer a lot of practical information – but also to share the personal experiences, needs and problems of carers today. I have been a carer myself – caring for my father with motor neurone disease after my mother's death, for my dying mother-in-law, and most recently for my daughter who has M.E. In addition, I have supported several carers – including my mother who cared for my father until her death, and my sister whose husband suffered heart disease and died after a heart transplant. I have also supported several friends, including George and Eileen Carey whose own account of caring is included in the first part of this book. Many of the voices in the book come from those people. Others originate as responses to a questionnaire sent out to a small sample of carers. Apart from the more in-depth stories in Part 1, minor details have been changed to preserve anonymity and the names are fictitious.

In supporting carers there were occasions when I didn't know what to say or how much practical help to offer. It is therefore my hope that this book will be an encouragement to readers in the same circumstances.

Christians are called to love and to serve one another. It is therefore vital that we care for carers with the loving consideration they need and deserve. With an increasing number of handicapped, ill and elderly people being looked after in their homes, it is important that we have Jesus' caring heart, and that we understand the different 'aspects' of his caring ministry to support the carers in our own family, church and neighbourhood.

Some of us live as though burdens do not exist

and that carers don't have any. Are carers covering their pain and tears? Are they denying themselves the right to the emotions God has given them? Are they 'heavy laden' with the continuous daily routine? I believe many are, as these comments show so clearly:

> I wish people wouldn't assume that because I love my father and want to look after him I must be all right – it's hard to tell others that I am crying out inside for help and support.

> Caring for my ill husband is so hard when he is such a changed man – if only I could put the clock back.

God cares for his world and uses his church to demonstrate his compassion. Until Jesus comes again, we are called to be Jesus to one another, so let us look at how Jesus cared for others and learn from his ministry. 'Carry each other's burdens, and in this way you will fulfil the law of Christ' (Gal 6:2).

# PART 1

# *Carers Speak for Themselves*

# 2

# *A Reversed Relationship*

## by Eileen Carey

My parents were in their forties when I was born. Although they had thought they would be unable to have children, my sister had arrived three years before me – and what a shock I must have been to them, weighing in at 10lb. They were good, caring parents and I don't remember ever thinking they were old until my father had to take early retirement because of ill-health. I was only in my mid-twenties with a young, still uncompleted family. My father then died just six weeks after our third child was born, and my mother went totally to pieces. Suddenly I found myself with three children under three, in our first curacy, becoming the 'carer' for someone who had always cared for me. My mother did eventually recover enough to go back and live in her own home, but at the time spent many weeks with us, and we spent every day off visiting her. (My sister had emigrated to Canada two years before my father died so was unable to provide any practical support.)

This pattern of life continued until Mother fell and fractured her femur three years later. We thought it was the beginning of the end. She was in her late sixties, and the experience in hospital affected her mind. She became quite irrational and very confused. However, though she did recover from this accident, she lost confidence in her ability to live alone. She came out of hospital to be with us. Even when she did manage to spend some time in her own home, she was unsettled, and every decision had to be made for her. At this point, with Carey no. 4 on the way, my mother decided to join my sister in Canada and make her home there. We packed up and sold the home in which she had lived for thirty-five years, and it was a very sad moment for us and for her grandchildren when she disappeared into the departure lounge.

There had been a wonderful relationship between my mother and our three children. She had infinite patience with them, spending endless hours teaching them to read, and playing games with them. She had already been a prominent figure in their young lives.

Our fourth child was born six weeks after my mother's departure and she grew up not knowing that wonderful 'friend' – Granny – that the other three knew. The pattern for our lives with my mother changed. She spent eighteen months in Canada and then bought a twelve-month, open-ended ticket to England. She went back on almost the expiry date. So the pattern emerged: eighteen months in Canada, twelve months with us. It worked well for about five years and then it was obvious, as her eightieth birthday approached, that she spent all her time in Canada feeling homesick for England. Letters from my sister indi-cated that Mother was very confused and so the decision was made that she should come home to live with us.

I met her flight at Newcastle Airport and I heard my name over the tannoy to go to the Lounge to meet her. She was in a wheelchair, barely recognisable as my mother, and very confused. A totally different person from the one we had waved off eighteen months before, yet underneath the changed exterior there was that loving mother and grandmother who was now totally dependent on us.

At this time we were living in a seven-bedroomed vicarage in Durham, so we were fortunate to have plenty of space to accommodate my mother. Soon it became very obvious that she needed round-the-clock care. At that time our children were fifteen, thirteen, twelve and six years of age and my husband was Vicar of a very busy parish. The strain on us as a family was enormous. The three older children were wonderful, but often Mother did not know them and was unable to do anything for them. They looked after her, tried to stimulate her by playing simple card games, read to her and spent time just being with her and loving her. They listened to the same stories of the past over and over again. She had no memory at all of the present. One thing she still did was to read her Bible every night. A lifetime's habit was the one thread linking the past and present, taking her into the future. Her Christian faith was very real.

When she first came to live with us permanently I was able to take her shopping with me and to church on a Sunday morning. Ella, a member of the congregation, used to look after her every Wednesday for our day off so that we could spend some time together. Ella was ten years younger than Mother and as my mother's condition deteriorated, and the depth of care needed was greater, that bit of space became an oasis to live for through the other days. We were never able to thank Ella enough for her care and love for Mother, and her sensitivity to us for showing her Christian faith in this practical way.

There were others in the congregation who helped us to bear the load. The author of this book was my husband's part-time secretary and she showed great love and care towards us, particularly as Mother's condition deteriorated. I was unable to leave her on her own at all. When I walked out of the room she followed me – even to the toilet. She became incontinent so I had to make sure that I took her at regular intervals to the bathroom. Every morning I bathed and dressed her, helped her with her meals and at the end of the day undressed her and tucked her into bed. Sometimes she would wander down into an evening meeting in the dining room with only her nightdress on and accuse my husband of stealing her money.

A number of the congregation knew of the stress we were under. They had known Mother when she used to visit us and take an active part in church activities, and we received tremendous support. Different people used to come in and sit with her if there were school activities that I needed to attend with the children. To be able to take a holiday with the family, we used to book her into a local authority nursing home which kept a bed for that express purpose. She had enough of her own money to pay for that, otherwise we could not have done it. She always cried and pleaded with me not to leave her. It was only for the sake of the family that I was able to do it and it helped to know that some of the church family would visit her. Yet another expression of their loving support.

This deteriorating condition continued for about a year, but another trauma in the family began to change it. Elizabeth, then seven, was knocked over by a car, received a compound fracture of her right leg and was in hospital for a week. This meant I had to spend most of my time at the hospital. The doctor stepped in and had Mother hospitalised for a period in a geriatric ward as she was suffering from a prolapsed rectum herself. The hospital was only able to keep Mother for a short time, but it gave us time to devote to Elizabeth and get her on the way to recovery. However, she was in a full-length leg plaster for nine weeks and a knee-length walking plaster for five weeks. We survived the summer, but as time went on it became obvious that the strain of round-the-clock, increasingly strenuous care was taking its toll on the whole family. Elizabeth was going more and more to play and stay with her friends. Her friends did not like coming to the vicarage because Granny frightened them. I was having to rely increasingly on the help of the older children with the practical running of the home. Also at that stage I was unable to get to church because Mother was not able to go and not able to be left alone. Others were able to do less for her because full nursing care was becoming necessary. Mentally I felt I was beginning to crack. I was trying to juggle with so many jobs and doing none of them properly. Yet in the middle of all this was a confused old lady we all loved dearly. However, I found myself coming to the realisation that I could not go on indefinitely without more help.

Our local GP had been marvellous and the practice had supplied rubber sheets, incontinence pads and many other aids to try to improve the quality of the help we could give Mother. Still, at this point, I reached the depths. I could see the effect it was having on the children, particularly Andrew who had been six weeks old when my father died. There was a deep bond between him and Mother, and right up till the end, when she remembered no one else, she always remembered him. As she deteriorated he became more and more upset and eczema patches started to appear on his arms and legs. I knew then that I had to do something about the situation as, however much we wanted to, we had to admit we were unable to cope.

I went to my very understanding doctor and burst into tears in front of him. Once I managed to calm down I was able to explain that I could no longer cope with looking after Mother as it was having an adverse effect on the children, our ministry and my health. The wheels started to turn and within a very short time she was taken into the local geriatric hospital to be assessed by the geriatrician. Then she came home and we were offered intermittent care for her, which meant two weeks at home and one week in hospital. During the two weeks at home she had a few hours in the day centre at the same hospital two days a week. This arrangement just gave us a bit of breathing space to begin to live again. We were able to visit every day because the hospital was only about a mile away from the vicarage. These changes of surroundings made very little difference to Mother. She always begged us not to leave her, but often she did not know who we were. The wonderfully caring staff assured us she was quite happy when we were not there, or at least as happy as she would be anywhere.

After a few months of intermittent care, Mother was taken full time into hospital and we brought her out to the vicarage for Sunday tea or a birthday of one of the family. Over the months she became more frail and picked up many infections. Many times we thought we were going to lose her. The staff gave her tender loving care and I asked that she should not be vigorously treated for the infections but only given drugs if she had any pain. Amazingly she fought infection after infection without treatment and bounced back. However, in the summer of 1981, while we were on holiday, her condition deteriorated. After two weeks of not seeing her it was a real shock to see the change in her. Each of the children came in to see her and say goodbye, although the only spark of recognition was when she saw Andrew. My husband George and I stayed with her together and then during the evening we returned to the vicarage. I could not settle and knew I had to go back to the hospital. The staff kindly moved Mother into a side ward and I sat with her throughout the night, holding her hand. She was unconscious, but I talked to her and said the Lord's Prayer and twenty-third Psalm over and over again. I talked about the family and how much we would miss her, but that we would all meet again in the glorious hereafter. She slipped away at 6.45 am and I was able to cuddle and kiss her for the last time before going to tell the staff that she was dead.

The last hours of her life were very important to me and I needed to be with her to the end. She had brought me into the world and had nurtured and cared for me. Our roles over the latter years had been reversed and I had become the carer. Throughout these very difficult times I had the wholehearted support and love of my husband. He loved Mother and had infinite patience with her and gave me the heart to go on during the black days. We were supported by others from the Christian family who cared for us and our family. Through their support, those caring people enabled us to survive all the difficulties and traumas. I hope all six of us have gained in knowledge and understanding, having been there ourselves.

# 3
# *I Didn't Feel Forgotten*

## by David Taylor

'Of course, you realise it's spreading.' Our eyes
met across the consultant's office and in that
moment we knew the truth. Our last vestige of
hope had gone! Death had always been a possibility, but we had thought mostly about symptoms,
treatment and recovery. Now we had to think
about symptoms, treatment and death. From that
day Enid had four months to live and they were to
be the happiest months of our twenty-seven years
of marriage!

Enid accepted, immediately, that day by day she
would be able to do less and less and, between us,
as each difficulty arose, we worked out together
how to overcome it. This drew us closer together
and made the difficulties less fearsome. We
devised ways of adapting Enid's clothes so that she
could dress herself for a few weeks longer. We
devised a lean/push way of getting upstairs and a
lean/pull way of getting down; both involved quite
an intimate embrace and we enjoyed the cuddle!
One day, on the way down, she slipped out of my
arms and ended up sitting on the staircase.

Without a word she bumped the rest of the way down, and after that we slept downstairs.

I was never very good at cooking and it was hard for Enid when she had to hand over the kitchen to me, especially as our standard of eating plummeted. However, after a few weeks word got around and people started to cook for us. Do you know what they cooked? Cakes ... hundreds of them! We had both larder and freezer full of cakes. I never quite worked out how to deal with the misplaced zeal which brought cakes we couldn't eat from people we didn't even know.

Joan, however, was different. She brought us hot, cooked meals, ready to eat. My, how welcome they were! So, if you are cooking for someone in need, especially in this day of freezers and microwaves, the hot meal, ready to eat, is the one that will be appreciated.

As Enid's needs changed, so God provided for them. I have always been squeamish about burns and sores. I was the one who wobbled out of the first aid class, feeling faint, when slides of burns were being shown. But now Enid had sores and how much more convenient for me to dress them rather than to wait for the district nurse. Normally, I could not have looked at them, let alone dressed them, but God worked a miracle. He changed me and I was able to dress those sores for several weeks. When the need passed, the miracle came to an end and I reverted to my normal squeamish self.

Not only did God change me, he changed Edith's role. Edith had driven Enid to and from her out-patient treatment for the past year. We hadn't known her very well, but she turned up right at the beginning saying that God had told her to come and help. Ever since then, without fail, she had given up her morning on treatment day. Now the treatment was over and Edith's role changed from driver to administrator. Enid needed to have someone with her constantly and Edith arranged the rota when I was away. I didn't feel forgotten!

Our marriage had been marred by several upsets when my loyalties to wife and work had got out of balance. Now Enid needed me more and more and God solved the problem in grand style: I was given notice of dismissal from my job! As I worked out my notice I had more time at home and there was no doubt in my mind that wife came before work. For the first time I acknowledged that she was more important than anything else in my life. The effect was doubled because, at last, and perhaps for the first time in all those married years, Enid knew without doubt that she came first. During those few months I found what it was to love unconditionally and always putting Enid first. Just as St Paul promises in the Bible, Enid responded to this by becoming more beautiful in feature and in character. She never complained of her condition and she was always a source of joy to those who came to visit her.

She used to love me to wash her feet. On one occasion she asked me if I felt humiliated by such a menial task. 'Oh no, Enid, I enjoy it. I love to do it for you.'

'That's nice,' she said. 'I feel so privileged.' How remarkable that such a little task became a source of great joy to both of us!

We used to read the Bible together; we knew that Enid was going to be with Jesus when she died. She was a little concerned about the dying part, but she never doubted that the new life would be much better than the old. About a week before her death, a little crisis occurred in her condition and, that same day, we read of Jesus telling his disciples that he was going ahead to prepare a place for them in heaven and that, when all was ready, he would come for them. 'Do you think he's coming for me today?' Enid asked.

'No,' I answered, 'not today, but soon.'

'Yes,' she replied, 'soon,' and her expression was all joy, almost excitement.

Enid spent the last week of her life in a hospice. She felt very much at home there after an earlier trial period. The sense of peace and love was almost tangible and, of course, she knew the presence of the Lord as well. She felt loved and cared for and was ready to leave this world and go on to the next.

I was with her when she died. Afterwards, I went into the Sister's office to find out what to do next, and to my surprise found myself crying. The Sister let me hold her hand. I held it for several minutes and received from that simple contact so much warmth and understanding and assurance. I don't think she said much, but it was a lovely thing that she did for me. I pulled myself together, thanked her and went off at peace to register the death.

Back home for a toasted sandwich, and I found that the grapevine had been at work. Barry Kissell called to see me (he was the curate in our parish). Finding me at peace, he told me how to organise the funeral. I didn't even have to think, 'What do I do next?' I certainly didn't feel forgotten, even though, from that moment, the supply of cakes and hot meals ceased!

While I was making coffee for Barry, there came another knock at the door. Douglas and John had come, unannounced from Cheam on the other side of London to visit Enid. Arriving too late to see her they had come to visit me. No, I didn't feel forgotten. Was there anything they could do? I asked Douglas if I could join his walking party in Switzerland. 'Yes,' he said, 'there is just one single room left. It's the last vacancy we have.' How good is the Lord!

I went back to the hospice to collect Enid's things and they took me unawares when they asked me if I would like to see her. I didn't feel strongly either way, but it seemed churlish to refuse, so I said 'yes'. I am glad that I did.

She was laid out in the chapel looking beautiful and peaceful; 'waxen' was how I described her features later. I looked at her and didn't quite know what to do, so I kissed her and sat down facing her. The Sister left, closing the door behind her, while I was reflecting on that kiss. Of course she had been unresponsive – I had expected that – but she had also felt cold to the touch and, somehow, that said to me, 'She is not here. This is only her *old* body. Now she has a new one, her resurrection body.' From that moment I lost interest in her old body.

My eyes drifted to a crucifix on the altar and I saw Christ hanging on the cross. 'But he, too, is resurrected,' I thought, and I turned the crucifix to show the empty cross symbolising 'Christ risen', just as Enid's old body seemed to symbolise 'Enid risen'. I could look beyond the empty cross and beyond the body and see them together in glory. Joy flowed through me as I sang choruses and thanked God for his goodness.

That evening, while telephoning the news, I was invited by nearby friends to stay the night with them. I wasn't forgotten! Neither was I forgotten when the church was packed for Enid's farewell service. She had planned the service and she wanted it to be a time of peace and thanksgiving when everyone could share the sense of closeness to God that she had experienced so vividly during her last months. Our vicar, David Pytches, led the worship and I was able to tell people how sure Enid had been that she was going to heaven. The coffin was there, in accordance with tradition, but it meant nothing to me. The love of God and the love of the people meant everything.

While Enid was ill, I had made several attempts to find a new job, but nothing had come to fruition. Now, in the week after Enid's death, I was offered three separate jobs! It seemed that while Enid needed me, God would not let me become concerned with work, but now that she needed me no more, he showed his largesse. The world may say 'coincidence', but in this coincidence I see the hand of God. He hadn't forgotten me either!

The job that I accepted was in Manchester, and until I bought a house, I lived with my good friends David and Margaret Hallatt. David was Rector of a busy parish and Margaret was often alone in the evenings. She spent nearly six months letting me talk to her about Enid, about how we had coped together and about what I wanted to do now. She was superb; she listened, she commented, she asked questions, she drew me out. She even seemed to enjoy it!

Four years later this story came to an end. Enid had said, 'Do marry again if you want to.' It was a kind thought, but it had not seemed relevant at the time. Now, as Jenny came into my life, things began to look different and I was grateful for Enid's words. I hadn't been lonely while I was on my own – I had even improved my cooking a little bit! – but as Jenny became more and more important to me, I realised how much better and richer life would be with her, and eventually we were married.

No, I hadn't been forgotten!

# 4

## *God's Special Gift*

### by Julia Madgwick

Our eldest child, James, now nearly five years old, is mentally handicapped. He suffers from a very rare syndrome (known as Hypomelanosis of Ito) which can affect children with varying degrees of severity. In James' case it has meant that his development has been slow in all areas. He can say three words, although understands perhaps twenty or so and recognises situations and familiar people. He has been very slow to sit and crawl, due to 'floppiness' (which has gradually improved), and he is only now beginning to stand and take his first steps. He also has bouts of fits every few weeks, which are reasonably well controlled on medication. He is a cheerful little boy with a very sociable personality, and he has appealing looks, with fair hair and big blue eyes.

Initially, we were not aware that there was anything wrong with him. We did have a slight panic when he was one week old, because his head was (and still is) larger than average; but a brain scan was normal, and we were reassured. At this time the Lord gave us Psalm 121 for James, which was to be a real help in months to come.

> The Lord watches over you – the Lord is your shade at your right hand; the sun will not harm you by day, nor the moon by night. The Lord will keep you from all harm – he will watch over your life; the Lord will watch over your coming and going both now and for evermore (Ps 121:5–8).

So we knew right at the start of his life that God had his hand on James. He appeared to develop normally to begin with, but as the months went by he became noticeably behind in his development, and when he was eight months old he started having fits. The next few months were very difficult: James underwent a number of investigations (which all produced normal results), and we were watching him closely for signs of normal development, wondering if he would catch up. The paediatrician didn't commit herself as to whether he was 'slow' until he was one year old, by which time we were aware there was a definite problem. He was referred to another hospital for further tests, and eventually a diagnosis was made when he was about fifteen months. Having a definite diagnosis helped in that we knew his problem was neither an hereditary one, nor one in which his condition would deteriorate, yet it did not give any idea of long-term progress.

At this stage we were trying to come to terms with the fact that the baby we had thought to be normal was in fact mentally handicapped. The process was like a bereavement in that we had lost the normal baby we thought we had been given,

and while James' handicap did not affect our love
for him, coming to terms with it was a major
readjustment to make. Also, we had to cope with
the day-to-day stresses of looking after a handicapped child. My husband, Stephen, accepted it
much more quickly than I. While he grieved over it,
he did not kick against it in the way that I did. I think
he was also helped by having work as a distraction.

My emotions were mainly those of grief and
bereavement, but I also felt angry and resentful
towards God, because I felt we had been cheated
out of a normal child. Despite this, I knew at rock
bottom that God was in it (especially having Psalm
121 to cling on to) and that he had the right to do
whatever he chose. If that included giving us a
handicapped child, that was his prerogative.
Friends in the church were praying for us at that
time, and although I very much valued their prayer
support, I actually *felt* very unsupported both
emotionally and practically.

At this time I found it difficult to pray and read
the Bible; indeed just getting through the day was
often difficult. I felt that there was a pressure
(which I am sure was unintended, but there,
nevertheless) being put upon me to cope in a more
'spiritual' way, when what I was feeling was
mainly grief and despair. I found that I was unable
to express what I was feeling, because there
seemed to be expectations that I should be coping.
I did appreciate people praying, but what I longed
for was somebody to weep with me, to comfort me
and to help bear my burdens. Because this was not
forthcoming, it led to my feeling rejected and hurt.

In fact I found that my attitude towards the
church became resentful. When on a Sunday

morning people were worshipping and bringing words from God, my thoughts were more along the lines of, 'Stuff all this. Why doesn't somebody care about *me*?' Because I felt so low, I wasn't able to talk this through with people in the church, which perhaps caused many of them to think that I was coping and hence perpetuated the problem. I am not condoning my attitude – merely reporting it honestly. Since that time I have had to confess it and put relationships right. In fact, ladies in the church were very receptive and understanding when I shared how I had felt hurt and rejected. I think that the problems arose for several reasons:

1. Not fully understanding the depth of grief experienced by both of us; to me it was like losing a baby.
2. They felt inadequate and didn't know what to do to help me.
3. They didn't know how to cope with James, and how to relate to him. One person admitted that she wanted to help look after him, but was scared that he would have a fit and die on her.

I think the major messages that needed to be heard and understood for people to be able to help were:

1. I needed to be accepted exactly where I was, without any spiritual demands being made upon me. I may well have been slow to listen to God and to let go of my anger, but God was well able to cope with that, and let me go at my own pace!
2. I didn't want people to come up with answers; I just wanted them to listen and show that they cared, and were prepared to hurt with me. That

didn't necessarily mean having an intense heart-to-heart. An arm around me or a word of encouragement also helped.

On a positive note, there were various ways in which we were helped and encouraged. We had some good friends who prayed with us regularly and were prepared to wrestle with us over the problems of 'Why?', 'What is God saying?', 'How do we pray – do we ask for healing?', and so on. God used them to bring words of encouragement about James, and the fact that there was a definite purpose for his life.

I was also very fortunate to have a Christian GP who listened to me and did not have expectations of how I should behave. I think this helped me not to feel guilty about the way I was coping; in fact he would encourage me by saying that he thought I was doing all right. Also, I had a couple of friends who took it in hand to have James one afternoon a week. This was especially helpful as I was expecting our second child at the time, and needed to rest. Little things, like people saying positive things about James, and being prepared to accept him, also helped. Conversely, one or two friends with normal children occasionally used to gush about the wonderful things their children could do, which was sometimes less than sensitive.

Since those early days the emotional hurt has been healed; it took me about two years to come to terms with James' handicap. The healing has partly been through the passage of time and partly through people's prayers. We were also greatly helped by the Lord giving us a little girl, Alice, whose rapid and normal development has been a real delight over the past three years. In giving her to us I feel that God has given back to us what we had lost with James. We now very much accept that James is God's special gift to us and he delights us in his own way. We have long since stopped comparing him with other children and know that God has a special path for him. And, of course, any new achievement by him is a source of delight.

Although the initial trauma is behind us, there are areas in which we feel the need for support. Living with a handicapped child brings its own stresses, and the routine of caring for him, helping him feed, changing his nappies can all be quite draining. Inevitably there are constraints put on the things we can do together as a family. There are also greater demands put upon my husband's time as I need more help in caring for James than I would with a normal child, especially as James cannot really join in with normal household activities in the same way that Alice can. I think the major ways in which we feel people can care for us now are:

1. Emotional support: recognition of the fact that life can be difficult and stressful. One lady wrote a letter of encouragement earlier in the year, which we appreciated. Others encourage us by the positive things they say about James. One example of this occurred shortly after James started at the nursery department of the local special school. One of his teachers described him as a 'ray of sunshine', which was lovely, especially as we do pray that James will bring something of God's love to those he comes into

contact with. I feel there needs to be ongoing recognition of the pressures put upon Stephen's time when there are other needs and demands from church and work.

2. Spiritual support: we have several friends who pray for James, and whom we can contact if there are bad times. There are times when he is miserable and fusses a lot, especially if he is going through a bout of fits, and it helps to share when the going is tough. Also, prayer for specific aspects of his life and development is appreciated.

3. Practical support: God has provided different people over the last few years to help look after James, or to help with housework. He now goes full time to the local special school (which he loves) and has some respite care regularly. All of these things have been a big help. At present our third baby is due imminently, and I have had several ladies who have helped me with ironing, etc. When James goes through a patch of fits, he is very miserable and needs a lot of cuddling. With an active little girl around this can be difficult. I have had help with Alice at these times, and having recently talked things through with several people in the church, I am sure that help with James at these times will be forthcoming. The main thing is that the need has to be identified and recognised. I am now much more able to ask for prayer and practical support.

God has taught us much through our little chap, and we are grateful for him. We are learning to cope with the stresses and problems, although obviously these will change as he gets older. I believe encouragement, prayer support and practical help are going to be long-term, ongoing needs with which the church can help, and in this way it will care and share and bear our burden with us.

# 5
# *Who Asks, 'How Are You, Steve?'?*

## by Steve Hepden

Who could have realised in early 1971, when my wife Chris went to the doctor with a slight numbness and tingling in her left hand and wrist, that twenty years later multiple sclerosis would still be trying to attack her body through her nervous system?

I will never forget that day. Halfway through the morning a doctor phoned me at the office to say my wife was very ill and I should come home immediately as a consultant was coming to examine her. Can you imagine what went through my mind as I raced through the traffic? Was she dying?

We were young and naive – I was twenty-six, Chris twenty-five, and our first child a few months old. We didn't have a clue what was going on. The doctor met me at the door and said in a 'stage whisper': 'She has MS.' I didn't understand. Chris immediately became very fearful: the only person she had known with the disease died at a very early age. Within a couple of hours Chris was in hospital, paralysed down her left side.

In 1981 I left my job as a chartered surveyor to

work in a church in Bristol. As well as being in the leadership team, I preach and teach here and abroad. So much about caring and the carer has come into focus since that time. In general I believe carers have been neglected. Christians are usually excellent in the short-term response, but even in a lively, thriving church, both carer and sick person can begin to feel lonely and isolated as people get taken up with other valid issues.

Over the years Chris has slowly declined, until today she is just about mobile around the house. How do I feel as a carer?

First, there was the struggle to come to terms with the reality of Chris's illness: she is ill every moment of every day. Sometimes she has even found it hard to get out of bed. When I travel, the pressure is still there. For many years my problem was that I could not cope, yet I had to. Life goes on, so there was conflict. I found it easy to click into unreality. I didn't want her ill, I couldn't cope with it, so I tried to ignore it. Often I hurt Chris by my words and 'faithlike' encouragement, which wasn't faith at all but a reaction which tried to make her live normally. When she couldn't I would become frustrated and she would get upset. Once, about ten years ago, I walked off and left her stranded in the shopping centre. We were shopping and her legs decided not to work. In a pique of frustration I walked away from her. I couldn't cope, so I copped out. The problem wasn't Chris but me. Over the years I have learned that I, as well as Chris, need to face the illness. Every day I need to cope. Nobody told me this, so over the years we have had to work it through the hard way.

In 1989 I was tested in a way that nearly finished

me off. I can now actually say 'multiple sclerosis', which is a breakthrough, but to accept Chris in a wheelchair? Never! For two or three years it had been clear that she was housebound. If we went shopping I would attempt to drop her outside the shop or perhaps park the car and then slowly walk her round. Chris would tire and I would encourage her to let me take her home. When one of our GPs started to talk about a wheelchair I backed off. Chris coped much better than I did. The week we got the chair we took a holiday and had some fun with it.

Secondly, there have been problems to face with our immediate family. I may be primarily a carer to Chris, but I am also a carer to my daughters. There are frustrations in every family, but growing up never knowing a fully healthy mum is difficult. In some areas – shopping for instance – I have had to be both father and mother to the girls – Joanna, now twenty, and Zoe, sixteen. We have always been honest with them about our feelings, and they are very aware that Christians are not immune to pressure and trouble, whether sickness or anything else. Pressure *can* be used for the good of the family. My role has been to bring peace to the girls' frustrations as they see their mum struggling. We have encouraged them to look outwards, bearing in mind the pressures in our own home, and they have begun to see the world from a caring perspective.

I also have to cope in the close family context with Chris's own frustrations when she sees us struggling and can do nothing to help. This can be destructive, particularly if I don't pick it up quickly.

Thirdly – coping in a church context. We are in a

young fellowship, with most people under thirty-five years of age; older people often seem to understand better. In general we have been helped consistently on a practical level – with cleaning, cakes and meals. One lady has taken the ironing weekly for the past three years, and many have prayed. In the leadership team there is great love and commitment, and help is always available. However, there is one area that does affect me as a carer: everywhere I go, people ask how Chris is, but never, *'How are you, Steve?'* I don't think people mean it; they just don't realise. People are so kind, but no one really thinks to look after me. When I struggle I need to take the initiative and ask for help, and I do, but sometimes I long for someone to look me in the eyes, ask a lot of questions and even give me a cuddle! Chris feels that people are doing all they can for her, and I agree, but I would like to be able to say the same about me. There certainly is a tension when you are in a loving, caring church and yet still sometimes feel lonely and isolated.

Fourthly – coping as a carer in terms of my ministry. Everywhere I go people know about Chris, mostly because I've told them. People listen to me when they realise that I have problems as well. They open up to the Holy Spirit and dramatic things happen – including people being healed. Sometimes, though, seeing many blessed by God does affect me. Why not Chris? I need caring for as much as Chris does.

It is my relationship with God that has sustained me. I love him, he is my Father and I know he cares for me. I can now trust God on Chris's behalf every day. I haven't always been able to do this. I remember once I felt resentful and was becoming bitter. I went to my fellow leaders and they helped me through. Amid the tears I saw that God does care, and he copes with my problems. I have friends to whom I can let things out, and that keeps me sane. I think I am discovering another side to God: I am learning that he is true to his word, and even when I don't feel him, he's there.

# 6

## *Torn Apart*

### by Jean Tame

For as long as I can remember, my father was ill, suffering from chronic bronchitis and emphysema (a disease of the lungs causing breathing difficulties). For years he needed constant care, day and night. This was given by my mother and inevitably took its toll on her health. It's perhaps not surprising that, growing up with this background, I ended up working for twenty-four years in the caring professions myself. My experience included adolescent units, children's homes, a unit for the physically and mentally handicapped, and finally working with the elderly.

Holding positions of responsibility in jobs like these meant that I could never be certain of getting the time off I was entitled to, simply because if other staff were sick, someone had to cover for them. Staying beyond my allotted time on duty was not done in a spirit of martyrdom but out of sheer necessity: people have to be cared for twenty-four hours a day, seven days a week. However, over the years, constant shift work and the stress of never knowing for sure that I would be able to take my time off affected my health.

The pressure on me from my work was not helped by the situation I was returning to at home: as the years went by my father became increasingly demanding and difficult. I would come home from 'caring' at work and immediately take over caring for Father, in order to give my mother a much needed break. This meant that I never had a proper break myself, and, as I am single, neither my parents nor the rest of the family ever seemed to think that I could possibly have anything else to do apart from holding the fort at home! Looking back now I can see that I perhaps contributed to this misapprehension by feeling myself that I was somehow responsible for covering my parents' every waking moment, so that Mother would manage while I was at work.

Inevitably, of course, I came to the end of my resources, both physically and emotionally. It is easy to be wise after the event and I know now that I should have been firmer about time off for myself, but it's very difficult to be detached and stand back when your own parents are in desperate need of help.

In June 1989 a close friend, who is a co-ordinator for CARE Trust, suggested I should try to have a break and visit a CARE home. I was in no fit state to travel far, and the thought of organising myself to get away was almost too much, despite my need of a few days away. Fortunately, a suitable CARE home just twenty miles away was suggested, so I made a big effort and took myself off for a week to a family in Sussex.

What they did for me was perfect: they left me

alone! I needed time just to be me, and I spent ages simply enjoying the garden. I went to bed when I wanted to, and, more importantly, got up when I wanted to. No questions were asked and no pressure was put on me. If I went out that was fine, if I stayed in that was fine too. (People sometimes find it difficult if someone goes out alone – but that was just what I needed at the time.)

At the end of the first week I was invited to stay for another week. Although I didn't realise it then, this was a valuable help to my recovery. I was relaxed because I felt the family didn't think they had to 'entertain' me. It meant a great deal to me to have time to stop and think, time just to 'be', since my life otherwise was, and is, very full and organised.

I shall always be grateful to CARE Trust for putting me in touch with that family, who simply loved and welcomed me and gave me the time and space I so desperately needed.

# PART 2

# *How to Care for a Carer*

# 7

## *Jesus the Carer*

**C** Compassion
**A** Awareness
**R** Response
**I** Initiative
**N** Needs
**G** Getting alongside

## Compassion

One of the greatest aspects of Jesus' ministry was his willingness to enter into the human situation and allow himself to feel its poignancy. The resulting compassion that rose up within him compelled him to help and heal. Compassion comes from a Greek word meaning 'to be moved in the depths of one's being' and suggests that as Christ was profoundly touched inwardly – at the depths of his emotions – energy was released so that he reached out and helped.

He was moved by the spiritual lostness of the crowd: 'He had compassion on them, because they were *harassed* and *helpless*, like sheep without a shepherd' (Mt 9:36, italics mine).

The sight of the sick touched him: 'When Jesus landed and saw a large crowd, he had compassion on them and healed their *sick*' (Mt 14:14, italics mine).

He felt for the physical needs of the hungry and tired crowd: 'I have compassion for these people; they have already been with me three days and have nothing to eat. I do not want to send them away *hungry*, or they may collapse on the way' (Mt 15:32, italics mine).

The plight of the two blind men moved him. 'Jesus had compassion on them and touched their eyes. Immediately they received their sight and followed him' (Mt 20:34).

He responded to the appeal of a leper: 'Filled with compassion, Jesus reached out his hand and touched the man' (Mk 1:41–42).

In Nain he experienced in his heart the pain of bereavement: 'As he approached the town gate, a dead person was being carried out – the only son of his mother, and she was a widow ... When the Lord saw her, *his heart went out to her*, and he said, "Don't cry"' (Lk 7:12–13, italics mine).

It was compassion welling up within Jesus that motivated him to care for those who were lost and helpless, sick, blind, hungry or bereaved. Many carers will feel lost and helpless in carrying through their responsibilities; others will be sick with the physical and emotional strain of caring for a loved one; some will be blind to what they can do and feel trapped in a dark corner; many will long for a respite from care, for a change of scenery, for a listening ear and for the knowledge that they are as important as their dependants; a few carers will already be grieving for the loss of a relationship as their dependants deteriorate. Our response to those in this situation must be one of love as we remind ourselves of the ministry of Jesus, of whom it is so often said, 'He was moved with compassion.'

## Awareness

Jesus had the wonderful gift of always being aware of people who were in need; he was able to minister right to the heart of a problem. He was aware not only of the spiritual needs of people, but also of the resources available to help people on a practical level.

The disciples came to Jesus asking how they could feed the 4000 hungry followers: 'Where could we get enough bread in this remote place to feed such a crowd?' Jesus asked, 'How many loaves do you have?' He became aware of the resources available, 'then he took the seven loaves and the fish, and when he had given thanks, he broke them and gave them to the disciples, and they in turn to the people. They all ate and were satisfied' (Mt 15:33–34, 36–37).

Similarly, Jesus was aware of the resources available when he fed the 5000.

Jesus replied,


'… You give them something to eat.'

'We have here only five loaves of bread and two fish,' they answered.

'Bring them here to me,' he said … Taking the five loaves and the two fish and looking up to heaven, he

gave thanks and broke the loaves. Then he gave them
to the disciples, and the disciples gave them to the
people. They all ate and were satisfied (Mt 14:16–20).

If we are to take Jesus' love to those who are
carers, then we too need to be aware of the
resources available to help people in practical
ways. There may be many occasions when we feel
that what we have to offer is of little significance,
but if like Jesus we thank God for the resources we
have, he will bless and use them. As we reach out
and offer the little we have, God will use us to help
and support others.

Jesus was not only aware of how people felt and
the resources available to help them, he was also
acutely aware of his relationship with his Father.
Jesus was always in touch with his Father, aware of
what the Father was doing and wanted done, and
relying totally on him. 'I tell you the truth, the Son
can do nothing by himself; he can do only what he
sees his Father doing, because whatever the Father
does the Son also does' (Jn 5:19). 'I do nothing on
my own but speak just what the Father has taught
me ... for I always do what pleases him' (Jn
8:28–29).

In the same way, it is crucial for us to be aware of
what God is doing and wants done in a particular
situation to help carers. It is vitally important that
our caring for carers grows out of a relationship
with God so that we stand on Jesus' words: 'I seek
not to please myself but him who sent me' (Jn
5:30).

## Response

Jesus responded to those in need by becoming personally involved in their situation. The story of the Good Samaritan (Lk 10:30–35) demonstrates this. Note that the Samaritan's compassion arose from seeing the victim in difficulties. Then the Samaritan took practical action, involving himself with immediate help. 'He put the man on his own donkey, brought him to an inn and took care of him.' His first action was to sort out something short term (the bandages and liniments), before making a long-term practical arrangement. 'The next day he took out two silver coins and gave them to the inn-keeper. 'Look after him,' he said, 'and when I return, I will reimburse you for any extra expense you may have.'

This story demonstrates three stages of getting involved with carers:

1. He *saw* him. We will know people caring for dependants, and it is important to see and understand their situation.
2. He *took pity*. We need to be open enough to allow God to move us with compassion for carers.
3. He *went* to him. We must get involved.

After Jesus had told this story to a law teacher, he commanded: 'Go and do likewise' (Lk 10:37).


## Initiative

When people were in a vulnerable position, Jesus often used his initiative and took the first step in helping them; he didn't always wait for people to ask for help.

After the disciples told Jesus about Simon's mother-in-law who was ill in bed with a fever, Jesus took the initiative: 'He went to her, took her hand and helped her up' (Mk 1:31).

Note how Jesus took command of the entire situation when he arrived at the house of Jairus' daughter, having heard of her death. 'He did not let anyone go in with him except Peter, John and James, and the child's father and mother.' After raising her from death, he 'told them to give her something to eat' (Lk 8:51, 55). Jesus took the initiative in organising the family, suggesting the little girl should be fed.

When the disciples were in difficulties in the middle of a lake on their way to Bethsaida Jesus saw them 'straining at the oars, because the wind was against them'. He made the first move:

> About the fourth watch of the night he went out to them, walking on the lake ... They cried out, because they all saw him and were terrified. Immediately he spoke to them and said, 'Take courage! It is I. Don't be afraid.' Then he climbed into the boat with them, and the wind died down (Mk 6:48–51).

Jesus used his initiative to help Zacchaeus come to self-acceptance and new life. It seems that Zacchaeus was fascinated by Jesus and so determined to see him that he climbed a tree. 'When Jesus reached the spot, he looked up' undoubtedly saw him sitting in the tree, and said to him, 'Zacchaeus, come down immediately. I must stay at your house today' (Lk 19:5). The initiative belongs to Jesus. He used it to see Zacchaeus not as an unacceptable tax collector but as a human being bruised and hurt by the circumstances of life and therefore a prime candidate for his love and acceptance. Jesus' presence in Zacchaeus' house was enough to give him new life and a new purpose in living.

When people are caring for others they do not always readily ask for help, so we need to use our initiative to get involved as and where God wants. Some carers feel they are drowning in the emotional strain, and need to hear the exhortation, 'Take courage, don't be afraid,' as we walk alongside them in this situation, offering emotional support. Using our initiative may result in our organising some practical support to bring love and acceptance to a carer.

## Needs

Jesus ministered to people's needs (physical, emotional and spiritual). When Jesus saw the paralysed man he first met his spiritual needs: 'Son, your sins are forgiven,' and then met his physical needs by healing him: 'I tell you, get up, take your mat and go home' (Mk 2:5–12). The man walked away physically and emotionally healed.

Jesus knew exactly how thoughts and attitudes affected a person's physiological functioning. His purpose was to bring people into greater 'wholeness'. This word implies completeness, maturity, and suggests an integrated, well-balanced, stable person. God has designed three parts of our being – spirit, soul and body – to interact with each other. 'May God himself sanctify you through and through. May your whole spirit, soul and body be kept blameless at the coming of our Lord Jesus Christ' (1 Thess 5:23).

'The spirit of man is the lamp of the Lord, searching all of the innermost parts of his being' (Prov 20:27, RSV). The Spirit of God mingles with our spirit so that the 'rivers of living water' that Jesus spoke of find release into our lives. In caring for carers, we need to be channels of life from God, reaching people's spirits, which will then affect their souls and bodies.

As Jesus ministered to the whole person he met emotional needs. The woman caught in adultery was released from the emotion of guilt when Jesus said to her, 'Neither do I condemn you ... Go now and leave your life of sin' (Jn 8:11).

Jesus' practical help revealed his love for the whole person. When the wine ran out at the wedding in Cana, he demonstrated his concern by telling the servants to 'fill the jars with water ... now draw some out and take it to the master of the banquet. They did so, and the master of the banquet tasted the water that had been turned into wine.' By doing something practical about a potentially embarrassing situation Jesus 'revealed his glory, and his disciples put their faith in him' (Jn 2:7–9, 11).

When caring for carers we will encounter many different needs and should act accordingly: performing practical tasks, offering a listening ear, helping the carer to set and achieve manageable goals, or ministering Christ's life-giving water into the dryness and emptiness of the carer's life.

## Getting alongside

The most wonderful example of Jesus getting alongside his sad and distraught disciples in an accepting and empathetic way was on the road to Emmaus, after his death. Quietly, and without any fuss, 'Jesus himself came up and walked along with them' (Lk 24:15). By gentle questioning and quiet listening, Jesus enabled the disciples to share their sadness. He asked them an open question – one that does not have a fixed answer. Such a question allows the exploration of one's inner thoughts and feelings, whereas a closed question is answered by a 'yes' or 'no'. He asked, 'What are you discussing together as you walk along?' The disciples replied, 'Are you the only one living in Jerusalem who doesn't know the things that have happened there in these days?' Jesus then asked for more clarification: 'What things?' (Lk 24:17–19). This open questioning enabled the disciples to dig a little deeper into their emotional turmoil. By giving them the space to recall and recount the events and experiences that were giving them pain, Jesus enabled the disciples to express their deep hurts and emotions. They had felt helpless to prevent Jesus' death; hurt because of what people had done to their best friend; grieved with the loss of the one they loved; hopeless and despairing because the one in whom they had put their hope was no longer alive; anger at the injustice of it all; and fear for their future. Through this experience of 'being listened to' the disciples acknowledged what was going on inside them and Jesus was able to minister to this sorrow-filled area of their experience.

We need to give our time and energies to getting

quietly alongside carers; to walking with them along their path; to listening and accepting them where they are; to allowing them the freedom to express how they feel. Only then will we be able to bring new light into their darkness, faith into their despair, and a hope for the future.

# 8

# *Thinking Things Through*

Caring involves people, feelings and relationships, and since there are many uncertainties it is good to encourage the carer to think things through. Many carers find themselves facing enormous difficulties through no fault of their own simply because, for one reason or another, they actually took on a carer's role without thinking things through initially. To discuss with them the way they organise their situations may help them see the value of changes which would enable them to cope better. As one such carer, Judith, remarked:

> I got out of the habit of thinking about myself. I hadn't got any energy left over for it. But it caught up on me. I can now see that it isn't wrong to think about myself.

Carers can't be superhuman and they need to be able to set realistic goals for themselves, so finding release from the burden of having to give time and energy from resources which they may not have. These carers had thought this through and adapted accordingly:

We love him and care for him as he is our child. But as parents we are also aware that if life had worked out differently he would be independent by now and our lives would be different. Therefore for our own sakes, we put limits on what we do.

## Keeping well

Encourage carers to look after their own health, as caring is hard work – physically and emotionally. Carers tend to ignore their own health needs and battle on, often deliberately not going to their GP to avoid possible admission to hospital. This is, however, very shortsighted – carers are much more likely to crack up without proper medical care themselves, and then two hospital beds are required instead of one! Carers should be encouraged to get all the medical treatment they need to keep fit and continue caring. Medical treatment may involve a visit to the hospital for a blood test, X-ray or physiotherapy, and here are opportunities for friends to relieve carers when they need treatment, and to give lifts to the hospital. If health problems arise, help the carer to look back and see how these might have been prevented so that the problem doesn't recur.

## The dependant's health

Carers need information about possible physiological and mental effects of a dependant's illness or disability, and how it can best be managed now, and in the future, so as to organise and plan sensibly. It may help to get information from specific national organisations for illnesses or disabilities. (See

Appendix 1 for list of addresses in the United Kingdom.)

The amount of information carers can handle depends on their personalities and temperaments. For some carers, information can be upsetting; the knowledge of what might (or might not) happen can be too heavy a burden to carry. Any information we obtain is almost always very general; no book or society can specifically say how an illness or disability will affect a particular individual. So some carers find the best way to cope is to live one day at a time rather than dwell too much on the 'facts' given by a doctor or society, as Joy commented:

> Just as well I didn't know that caring for my aged, senile father would last for ten years, from age seventy-five to eighty-five. If I had known that at the beginning I would have cracked under the strain.

## Organising the environment

When people first realise that they will be taking a carer's role it is important that their living environment is explored; caring in their own home may be very difficult if the home is unsuitable. It may not always be practical or easy to move house, but before deciding on any change the carer needs to think through the future. Rather than move, carers may be able to adapt their present homes. For example, it makes no sense to put a shower in the bathroom upstairs, if eventually the dependant will be nursed downstairs. The carer will undoubtedly find that the proximity of the toilet is a major factor in the decision about where someone will be cared for.

Other members of the household need to be taken into account when their living environment is considered. Providing physical as well as emotional space for the carer and her family as well as the dependant is vitally important for a sane household! Everybody needs space to get away from others at certain times, and if there is not much space in the home, carers may have to reorganise what is available. Accommodating everybody's needs will not just happen by chance; it needs discussion and working out what is fair for all concerned, including the carer. It is better to think and talk this through at an early stage than to let tension build up, and maybe the family would value an outsider at the family negotiations. This could help each member of the family to look at his needs objectively and to reach agreement.

Here is how one family solved the problem of space and privacy:

> Each of our children now has a lock on their bedroom door, as their privacy was often broken by my aged, senile mother, wandering in unannounced and uninvited. At least they can go somewhere quiet now and do their homework.

## Holidays

Just organising the home environment isn't enough – every carer needs a holiday! But the mere mention of holidays can provoke fear in the dependant and guilt in the carer – who may feel indispensable. However, friends and family can encourage the carer to consider the possibilities (practical suggestions for this are given in chapter 11). Naturally the dependant will continue to require care, and if possible some choices should be offered. Would they prefer to go into a local residential or nursing home for a short stay, or perhaps go to another relative or friend? Another option could be to stay at home and be cared for by someone else, perhaps a friend, relative or a paid live-in nurse or care assistant.

Some of these options involve financial considerations. State benefits (income support) are sometimes available to help pay for short-stay residential care. However, some elderly people are out of touch with current costs of care and therefore refuse to pay, even when they are well able to afford it. Some carers allow the Attendance Allowance (see Appendix) to accumulate for a few weeks and then use it to pay for respite care.

Under the new Children Act handicapped young people have an automatic right to respite care in a residential home or with a family to give their parents the chance of a holiday.

## Major changes

Sometimes the carer does not actually live with the dependent person because at present he or she does not require total care. In this situation encourage the carer to think through the future for everyone involved before taking on the full care of a dependant who will deteriorate. Talking it through with someone outside the family is more objective and the issues can be seen more logically. Encourage the carer to think of his own needs – is moving into the dependant's home the only and best answer? What responsibility do carers have to their own family? Whether or not they live in the same home, always encourage carers to talk things through with their dependants where appropriate to discover their needs, views and desires.

It is important to keep in mind that being ill or disabled doesn't necessarily mean that dependants cannot make decisions, and *taking* over should never be a substitute for talking over. Obviously, if the carer looks after a child or someone who is mentally ill this may not be possible, and in this situation the carer's need to be listened to is even greater. The extent to which the situation and feelings are talked through with the people they care for will depend on the relationships between carers and dependants. This is particularly important when major changes need to be made, and can avoid hurts and misunderstanding later.

One family explained what they did:

> We built a granny flat as an extension to our house and said to my aging parents that as a family we needed privacy and that they were never to walk into our house uninvited. Although this seemed a harsh thing to say it worked very well for as my parents became very disabled we ended up caring for them in their own flat rather than allowing the caring to affect our own family in our home.

## Maintaining independence

Carers may find themselves attempting the impossible by aiming to meet everybody's needs – often losing sight of their own in the process. If this happens it is worth talking through the whole situation with the carer, realising that there may not be one easy, magic solution, and that various approaches may need to be tried before a workable one is found. It may be helpful to talk through dependants' needs with carers and see if they are doing too much for them. It is often easier and quicker for carers to do things themselves, but they need to see the importance of encouraging old, ill or handicapped people to be independent for as long as possible. This is particularly important in the usual daily activities such as dressing, washing, toileting and feeding. If help is needed it is worth seeing whether the simple provision of a piece of equipment could increase independence. For example, lever taps are much easier for a person with arthritic hands. Alternatively a tap turner may solve this problem. A raised toilet seat or a grab rail on the wall may enable someone to be independent in the toilet, and thick handles on cutlery may enable someone to feed himself. The height of the dependant's bed is also very important. Nursing someone in a low bed will do lasting damage to a carer's back. District nurses sometimes ask for their patient to be in a higher bed. This can be achieved by raising the bed with housebricks.

Everyone uses an armchair, but for an elderly or disabled person there are other factors besides comfort to consider. The height of the seat and arms is crucial – much modern furniture is too low. A person's ability to rise unaided from his chair is worth spending money on to preserve the carer's back! A new armchair is a good investment; it is worth shopping around to get the right one.

## Residential care for young adults

Encouraging independence in an adult or child with special needs may mean looking at an entirely different solution such as accommodation that gives the dependant some independence yet at the same time also offers care and support.

Residential accommodation may be state-owned, voluntary or private. By looking in *Yellow Pages* (under residential/nursing homes) or contacting the Citizens Advice Bureau carers may find a local agency that gives advice about the private sector and explains the state benefit system. An agency can help a carer to find appropriate residential care. If she decides a residential home is best, encourage the carer to sit down with a professional and look at all the options: the whole field of residential care is very complicated (details of residential care for specific handicaps are given in chapter 9). One family who made this decision summed up their feelings like this:

> At home we were trying to achieve the impossible. Once she was away we felt so much freer that we had more energy to give to her in the long run.

## Residential care for the elderly

Agreeing to an elderly dependant going into a residential home is often a much harder decision for carers to take, but there may come a time when after thinking long and hard about their roles, carers decide that they cannot manage any longer. For example, when a senile person no longer knows where he is at home and doesn't recognise the person caring for him, it may be time to discuss alternatives and face the decision to apply for a residential home. At this stage we need to give carers a great deal of support in sticking to that decision and following it through.

They will be vulnerable to feelings of guilt at such times.

This conflict of feelings is illustrated by Vera:

> When he was younger and fitter he asked me never to put him into a home. Now he is ill with motor neurone disease, and dying a progressive death. I have come to the end of my tether – I can't cope. Yet I promised him ... what do I do?

Alternative care will invariably mean permanent care in some kind of home. Encourage carers to contact their local GP or social worker to find what is available. Depending on the local resources, the possibilities of residential accommodation may include:

A social service hostel or home

A residential or nursing home run by a voluntary organisation

A private residential or nursing home

Sheltered accommodation

Special accommodation with a housing association

Long-term care in hospital under the NHS

A hospice.

The final decision about caring is one of the most difficult steps for carers to take, and they need to see that what they are doing is not so much giving up, or handing over, as making different caring arrangements.

> Because I live miles away from my father I am not able to see him very often, but occasionally I can arrange

an extra week off work. Then I take him out of hospital and nurse him in his own home for that week. These are very special times, and it makes all the hard work of keeping on his empty home worthwhile as I see the joy it gives him to go home.

As pointed out at the beginning, many problems can be avoided or made less significant if carers are encouraged to think things through, given support in difficult decisions, and perhaps above all listened to. Often as people talk about a situation to somebody outside it, they can begin to see possible solutions for themselves. This listening takes time and energy, but if we are really to support carers we should be prepared to give them our time, in listening and in gathering relevant information for them.

# 9

## *Exploring Available Resources*

The services offered by the local authority and health services can be as diverse as carers' needs. What works well for carers in one area may not be available in another, and the local church could play a significant role in meeting needs not met by the local authority or health service. For example, churches might offer the resources of their buildings to be used as a day centre and the many pastoral contacts in the community can be utilised. As each congregation is unique in its strength and resources, so individual Christians will be able to offer through their fellowship different gifts for the support and help of carers. A group of churches in a village may want to pool available resources, whereas another church may want to contact the local authority to offer to facilitate a care scheme in its own area.

On the other hand, individual members of a church may become actively involved in voluntary bodies supporting and caring for others. In this way the church as a congregation of Christians can help break down the social stigma attached to disability and mental illness and thus support carers.

Ian's wife was mentally ill:

> I didn't know where to turn when my wife was taken into hospital. Although I am not a churchgoer I telephoned my local church and they found a family to look after my two boys after school until I arrived home from work.

A Christian organisation called Cause for Concern (see Appendix 1 for the address of this and all the other organisations mentioned in this chapter) is committed to encouraging the church to take a practical interest in people with mental handicap. Along with other Christian agencies they have produced a Christian Awareness Pack on Mental Handicap which has resulted from the 'Hand in Hand' initiative and it seeks to encourage the church to befriend the mentally handicapped and their carers. They are also in the process of preparing a volume for the CARE series, to which this book belongs, to help increase our awareness and understanding of the mentally handicapped.

It is, of course, important that churches do not set up in opposition to local services but rather work alongside them. Most local authorities work to a tight budget and while ready and able to help, they don't have the money to advertise their services so will rarely come knocking on the carer's door. We all need to be prepared to work hard therefore to get the service that carers need.

The district health authority manages the health services, whereas the local authority manages the social services, education and housing. Numerous charities also exist and these can often provide equipment and services if the local authority/social services are unable to help in a particular instance. It is always worth trying social services first, then one of the charities listed in this chapter. Everyone has a right to know what is available – wherever carers live there is always a core of services on offer – and the burden of exploring these can be taken from carers by friends. How can we find out what services are available and whom to contact?

The Citizens Advice Bureau often has an overall picture of local authority services and resources, so it is probably the first port of call. Staff there will also be able to inform carers of local voluntary or private resources. *Yellow Pages* and your *Thomson Local Directory* also list private sources of help under the headings of: Disabled, Home Help Services, Handicapped, Nurses and Nursing Agencies, etc. Health and local authority services are often over-stretched, so a long wait for an essential piece of equipment may be expected. Nursing equipment is available through private agencies, though of course all this can be expensive.

The Disabled Persons Act (Services, Consultation and Representation) 1986, states that the local authority, when requested, has a duty to assess the needs of a disabled person. They will assess needs for:

Equipment and adaptations

Holidays, meals and telephones

Recreational facilities both in and outside the home.

When the local authority makes the assessment, the ability of the carer to continue to provide care on a regular basis has to be taken into account.

## Adaptations to the home

To maintain as much independence as possible for the dependant, extra fixed equipment or alterations to the home itself may be the solution. A social worker or occupational therapist will offer help and advice about any fixed equipment, e.g. flashing lights for doorbell and telephone for the deaf, and any adaptations deemed necessary to the home. The local authority or social services often pays for equipment in any home and usually pays for structural alterations and adaptations to council houses; otherwise carers may have to apply for financial help or pay out of available financial resources. However, claims have to be made before any work is started. The Centre on Environment for the Handicapped gives free advice on extending or adapting a home to accommodate a disabled or elderly person. They are also able to recommend architects who have had experience in designing and adapting homes for the disabled.

One disabled person, John, spoke of the extra independence this gave him:

> I had the doors in my house widened so now I am able to be mobile in my wheelchair. What a difference it has made. I now feel I am more independent. Although it was a long wait, it was worth every minute.

Possible adaptations include:

Handrails next to the bath, lavatory or stairs

A stairgate

A ramp for wheelchair access to the house

Widening doors for a wheelchair

A WC/shower downstairs

A hoist over the bath

An extra room

A stairlift, or lift that will take a wheelchair.

## Equipment

A wide range of equipment is available to help the people being cared for to stay as independent as possible. Carers don't always know what will help until they know what is available. The DSS leaflet *Equipment for Disabled People* (code number HB2) gives more information about equipment. A certain piece of equipment can save so much energy wasted in struggling over a particular problem. Available equipment helps people in the day-to-day tasks of bathing, washing, dressing, cooking, eating, using the toilet, turning the pages of a book and many other procedures.

Enid, a wife, explained:

> My husband loved reading but had great difficulty in turning the pages. Many a time I would find him frustrated and near to tears as, in the process of trying to turn to the next page, the whole book had fallen to the floor and he couldn't pick it up. The equipment (borrowed from social services) which turned the pages for him gave him a new lease of life.

Equipment can also be obtained through contacting the primary health care team (see chapter 10).

## Laundry services

If laundry services are available locally they will probably be run either by the social services department or occasionally by the district health authority. There is usually a small charge for this service, which launders bed linen for those suffering with incontinence. Occasionally they may launder the clothes of people who are too disabled or ill to manage to wash their own. The district nurse, GP or social worker will be able to advise about local laundry services. Another route is contacting the social services department or district health authority.

Family Fund gives information about what is available for a severely physically or mentally handicapped child under the age of sixteen years in the way of a washing machine, bedding, clothing, special equipment, etc. Application for money from the Family Fund must be made on a special application form available from Family Fund. If there are heavy laundry needs and the carer or his dependant qualifies for income support, the DSS may pay something towards a washing machine.

## Continence advisers

The district nurse should be able to advise about the availability of a local continence adviser. Such a person works within the district health authority and can:

Assess for incontinence problems

Treat incontinence (where possible)

Give practical advice on managing incontinence

Inform and advise about incontinence pads, special pants, etc.

The Association of Continence Advisers at the Disabled Living Foundation will give helpful advice.

## Night-time care

Very few schemes offer care during the night, and the main help may come from family, friends or neighbours taking over for the odd night – so this is where Christians can definitely help. Private agencies offer night-time care, but again this can be very expensive.

## Meals on Wheels

Meals on Wheels offers a voluntary service providing hot meals for people not able to cook for themselves. Depending on the local scheme, meals may be offered daily during the week, two or three times a week, and occasionally at weekends. However, in many areas the service is not available at weekends. This is an ideal opportunity for a local church to meet a very practical need: providing an extra hot meal or two on Saturdays or Sundays really takes very little effort, yet means so much to the carer and dependant.

The Meals on Wheels service provides a midday meal for a disabled or elderly person whose carer is out at work all day. It may also provide a meal if on any occasion the carer is ill and thus unable to cook for the dependant – in this instance a meal may be available for the carer as well as for the person cared for. A nominal charge is usually made. If someone qualifies for Meals on Wheels, the local social services department or GP should be able to give relevant information and a contact telephone number.

This service can make an enormous difference to the quality of a carer's own life. Elizabeth says:

> Meals on Wheels has made such a difference to me as they provide a meal every Monday, Wednesday and Friday. I don't any longer feel guilty that I am not providing for my father on those days, and I am free to get away and have lunch with a friend, or go shopping. It's lifted a weight off my shoulders – I now have a few days when I am free.

In some areas private enterprises have set up their own meals on wheels service, but some of these operate on a commercial basis. There is also an increasing hot meal service from take-away restaurants, but again this may be expensive.

### Educational resources

In the United Kingdom the local education authority must provide free, full-time education for all children with special needs from five to sixteen years, and up to nineteen years if the student wishes to continue. If a child with special needs is under two years of age, his parents can request an assessment by the local education authority by writing to the director of education at the local education authority. If a child is over two years of age, the local education authority must make an assessment to discover the child's educational needs and offer advice about how to meet them. Parents have the right to be present throughout the assessment along with an educational psychologist, a medical person, perhaps a teacher (if the child is at school) and a social worker. If the child is declared to have special educational needs then a draft statement is issued, highlighting the child's needs and how they should be met. Parents have the right to see this draft statement and the opportunity to discuss it further with a named person in the local education authority if they feel it necessary. Before the statement is finalised, parents have the right to appeal or disagree with any part of the statement. Once a statement is finalised a yearly review comes into operation. If a child wishes to go on to college the statement no longer stands, so it may be in a child's interest to stay on at school after sixteen rather than change to college.

It is very important that parents are free to ask and challenge anything they are not sure about. Christians in education could make themselves available to parents in this situation to talk through issues, explain educational jargon and so on. Advisory Centre for Education offers advice and help by letter or telephone. It produces two helpful publications: *The Advisory Centre for Education Special Education Handbook* and *Under 5s with special needs*.

There are many different services for children of all ages with special needs varying according to area. Pre-school children with special needs may be able to go to:

A nursery

A nursery school

A playgroup

An opportunity group (a playgroup specifically for children with special needs).

Voluntary and local-education-authority home learning schemes are also available, where a teacher visits the child in the home and involves the carer and the child together, showing the carer how to extend the child's knowledge and mobility. Contact the local education authority and speak to the educational adviser for special needs for information on what is available along these lines.

In some areas toys suitable for children with special needs can be borrowed from toy libraries. Write to or telephone Play Matters/Toy Libraries for information.

School-age children may be able to go to an ordinary school, special school, use a home learning scheme or have a combination of these. More and more head teachers are willing to integrate children with special needs into ordinary schools, and in some areas the local education authority pays an educational assistant to go into a school specifically to look after a child with special needs. In other areas, this service is not available, but the head teacher may be very happy to accept a child with special needs provided the parents pay for a full-time carer while the child is in school. Besides schooling, the child may benefit from a recreational playgroup/club. The teacher may advise on local opportunities of this kind or the educational adviser for children with special needs at the local education authority may be able to help. MENCAP also runs special play schemes.

Various other schemes help integrate older children into society, but as already noted every child with special needs has the right to continue in education until the age of nineteen years. A disablement resettlement officer can be contacted at or through the local job centre. He or she helps young people find a suitable job, or advises on further training. Occasionally the officer may be able to find a suitable work centre or sheltered workshop where training, retraining or work experience in a protected environment is available. There may also be a specialist careers officer at the child's school who can give information about various schemes available to prepare young people for work. The National Bureau for Handicapped Students gives information on courses, allowances and grants. Disabled people can receive information from RADAR (the Royal Association for Disability And Rehabilitation) about what is available for the disabled, whereas MENCAP offers advice and information for those with mental handicap.

## Voluntary and private resources

*The Disabled Living Foundation* has about thirty-three permanent exhibitions (called disabled living centres) around the country. Most centres are open on a full-time basis, and have a comprehensive range of equipment, clothing, footwear, etc. Many also house specialist advice or support services concerning other aspects of daily living. An appointment booked in advance will ensure the benefit of high quality information or advice. A friend could sit with a dependant to enable the carer to visit this exhibition.

*The Spastics Society* organises a visiting aids/equipment centre where it demonstrates a whole range of equipment. For further details contact the Spastics Society.

*The Red Cross* also lends some equipment in return for a small donation.

*REMAP* (Technical Equipment for Disabled People) makes technical equipment to individual requirements for products that cannot be bought on the commercial market. There is rarely any charge as REMAP members work for nothing, often using unwanted and discarded industrial materials. REMAP receives generous practical help from private and government workshops as well as from education institutes.

*Keep Able* has a display of equipment for sale and will also give advice.

*Boots the Chemist* produces a free catalogue *Health Care in the Home* giving details of equipment it sells. Available from the pharmacy department of large stores.

*Healthlines* is a new mail-order catalogue offering a range of carefully selected products designed for practical application and quality, to give comfort and a healthier lifestyle to those people with special needs, and to carers.


## Residential homes

*MENCAP* gives information about homes for people with learning difficulties.

*RADAR* gives a list of housing associations with housing specially designed for disabled people.

*CAREMATCH* gives information on homes throughout the country for people aged sixteen to sixty-five with physical disabilities.

*CARESEARCH* gives details of homes for mentally handicapped people all over Britain.

With both CAREMATCH and CARESEARCH

requirements for a disabled or handicapped person are fed into a computer, and details of suitable homes are then sent out. These details do not specify which homes have places available.

## Sports and leisure

Many local authorities run special classes, e.g. swimming for the disabled, or offer discounts on entry fees. In addition, a variety of social groups exists, and many local societies have a programme of activities for the disabled, their families and friends.

### Library delivery service

Most local authorities have this service for the housebound, including the carers. Details can be obtained from the local library. Many libraries loan tapes and records.

### Large print and talking books

These are available for the blind and partially sighted from RNIB, Torch Trust for the Blind and some libraries. Torch Trust for the Blind is a Christian organisation providing Scripture, Christian books and other publications in large print and on tapes (catalogue available on request).

There is also a Talking Newspaper Association which makes available the latest news. BBC Radio 4 produces a guide to services for people with a visual handicap called *The 'In Touch' Handbook*.

### Riding for the Disabled Association

Many riding schools have specially trained staff to teach the disabled. Telephone the central office to obtain details of local riding schemes.

## Transport

The Department of Transport supplies an excellent free booklet called *Door to Door. A Guide to Transport for the Disabled* (see Appendix 2 for address). This booklet gives information for individual personal transport, including everything from walking frames, wheelchairs, cars, local buses, trains and taxis. It also gives wider information for long-distance travel by sea, air or coach as well as group transport, such as community buses, health authority and local authority.

The orange-badge scheme, which can be applied for through the Social Services Department, allows concessionary parking to be given to anyone aged two years and over who:

Is blind

Receives mobility allowance

Uses a vehicle supplied by a government department

Receives a grant towards their own vehicle

Has great difficulty in walking (a letter from their GP may be needed to confirm this).

### Public transport

The Disabled Person's Railcard leaflet gives information about concessions for British Rail fares, together with details of:

Access to stations

Seat reservations

Sleeper and motorail services

Toilets

Travelling in the guard's van.

The leaflet is available from local railway stations or from the British Railways Board (see Appendix 2 for address).

A Disabled Person's Railcard allows a disabled person and his carer to receive cheaper rail travel, as well as other concessions according to the time of year and area.

'Customer's care' is a service offered by British Rail which assists travellers in any need, for example, carrying cases, making arrangements for transportation of wheelchair and finding seating accommodation. Telephone your local railway station giving advance notification of help needed.

Many local transport authorities offer a public service to those who find it difficult to use ordinary public transport. A door-to-door service is available under many different names: Readibus, Dial-a-Ride, Ring and Ride, etc. Contact the local transport authority for local details, or London Dial-a-Ride Users' Association.

These services can be used for any social trips (as one would use the ordinary service), trips to work and further adult education or trips to connecting train and coach services, but not for hospital appointments. The buses have low steps and a passenger lift, so it's easy to get on and off with a wheelchair. Fares are similar to ordinary bus fares and in some areas bus tokens are accepted. The carer is able to accompany the dependant, and some schemes offer an escort for a small charge. How to register with one of these schemes will depend on its local rules, and an application form may have to be signed by a GP. A journey can be booked for a certain departure time, and the advance booking time will vary from one scheme to another.

One disabled user of such a scheme writes:

> The local authority transport for the disabled gives me the freedom to visit my daughter every week. It is so much more refreshing to leave the four walls of my home and visit her in hers. This is a weekly outing I wouldn't miss for anything.

*Help with Mobility: Getting Around* (HB 4) leaflet is available free from the Department of Social Security.

### Private transport

The Disabled Living Foundation and RADAR both give information and advice on such matters as:

Buying or leasing a specially adapted car

Adapting an existing car for the handicapped to drive

Adapting an existing car to take a dependant (e.g. to fit a car to take a wheelchair or a special harness for a mentally handicapped child).

Free information on transport is given by the Mobility Advice and Vehicle Information Service. The dependant can only use this scheme if he receives a mobility allowance. They offer the following services where a fee is payable:

Assess and advise new drivers or newly-disabled people who want to drive

Give advice on car adaptations for drivers and passengers

Sessions to help people learn how to use their new vehicle.

A company called Assistance and Independence for Disabled People offers disabled people an opportunity to buy their own cars on hire purchase, on a no-deposit basis. As this is a private commercial company anyone can use it, with insurance and a special emergency rescue service offered on many models which are adapted to special needs. Delivery can be arranged.

Motability is a voluntary organisation which helps and advises the disabled with a leasing and hire purchasing scheme if they want to use their mobility allowance to buy or lease a car.

For a membership fee the Disabled Drivers' Association and the Disabled Drivers' Motor Club offer advice about car conversions. Members of the Disabled Drivers' Motor Club are also entitled to special benefits and allowances, enjoying concessions on car ferries, discounts on disabled drivers' car insurance and on RAC membership. The Disabled Drivers' Association has social gatherings throughout the country and campaigns for better local access for disabled people.

*Voluntary organisations*

Local voluntary organisations may be able to help with transport. Social care schemes may be available where a volunteer uses his or her car to take dependant and carer (if necessary) to wherever they want to go. A nominal fee is often charged.

To find out what is offered in your local area, contact the council for voluntary services. The telephone number may be found in the phone book under this heading or 'Voluntary Action Group' or 'Volunteer Bureau'.

## Toilets for disabled people

Throughout the country are locked disabled people's toilets only accessible by the use of a special key. RADAR supplies these keys at a cost together with a list of toilet locations.

## Useful publications

Information to help with managing difficult and confused behaviour, as well as other general information for the carer, can be obtained from several sources. For a list of some of the most helpful please see Appendix 2 of this book.

# 10

# *Knowing the Key Workers*

Many different people will have important roles in helping the carer with the dependant. Understanding the key workers' boundaries of responsibility helps carers to obtain the services they need. In turn, through understanding the worker's role, a good relationship can be built in which carers are free to talk and ask questions.

The primary health care team is the main body of people responsible for the health care of a dependant. That team comprises GPs, district nurses, health visitors and occasionally a counsellor.

## Doctors – GPs

A GP's role is not only to provide health care, but also to give information, advice and support. An understanding GP is worth his weight in gold in his ability to release other members of the primary health care team to support the carer in caring. Lesley found her GP particularly caring:

My husband and I had been with the same GP for fifteen years and when we found out my husband had a muscle wasting disease, our doctor immediately visited and gave us his time and attention. He made himself available to us, so that we felt free to take whatever worries we had to him whether they were big or small. Nothing was too much trouble. He also organised the visits of the district and auxiliary nurses – we didn't have to ask, he took the initiative.

GPs can support the carers' requests for a home help, attendance allowance, mobility allowance, day care attendance, residential care, sheltered accommodation, short breaks or holidays. If carers are unhappy about their own GP, or about the GP responsible for the dependant, they may need to think about taking steps to move to another practice. It isn't difficult to change GP, but the first step is to 'shop around', asking advice from local friends, to find a GP who offers what the carer needs. Remind carers that essential services offered by GPs are:

Easy, accessible appointment systems

Convenient surgery hours

GPs prepared to do home visits, and even to visit unasked out of genuine care for the patient

Willingness to offer time to listen

Other members of the primary health care team such as nurses, health visitors, counsellors. A few surgeries have practice visitors

Premises with wheelchair access

Similar cultural background to majority of patients.

If the carer decides (maybe in consultation with the dependant) to change surgeries, she should contact the new GP and ask if a change is possible. Rather than criticise the old GP it is better to give a genuine reason for changing: the hours are better, there is access for a wheelchair, they want a woman doctor, etc. If the new GP decides to accept the patient the carer can simply register him at the surgery with his medical card. Remember that elderly patients are often devoted to equally elderly GPs and will suffer no other!

## District nurses

District nurses, important members of the primary health care team, have been especially trained to nurse people in their homes. They visit regularly and carry out bathing, lifting, turning and other medical procedures such as changing dressings and giving injections. They have access to many home appliances such as commodes and crutches, and will advise on managing incontinence. Not only will they carry out nursing duties, but they will also advise and teach carers how to do these things. Depending on what services are available they may be able to arrange the following:

Bed rails, or a special bed for whatever reason

An electric chair or manual hoist above a bed/bath

A 'ripple' mattress or a sheepskin to prevent bed sores

A bath seat

A commode or urinal

Incontinence pads, drawsheets, pants, etc

Possible laundry service

Visit from a continence adviser (see chapter 9)

An auxiliary nurse to help bathe the dependant.

The difference such visits can make to the quality of a carer's life is clearly demonstrated in this example:

> Our district nurse came in three times a week to give my husband a shower, so that I had a rest from that job on those days. She became as dear to us as a family visitor; our day was brightened up by her visit – she couldn't have been more helpful with giving us a listening ear and advice on how to manage to get my husband out of bed in the mornings. He was too heavy to be lifted, but she showed me how to manage him.

## Health visitors

Health visitors, usually attached to primary health care teams, are nurses trained to work in families with special needs. They don't get involved in any practical nursing, but can:

Inform carers about local services, both statutory and voluntary, and help make contacts

Advise on benefits (see Appendix 3)

Help arrange for home adaptations and equipment

A health visitor is somebody to talk to, to offload onto and get advice from. Like the district nurse, she often acts as a link between the carer and GP.

Carers can be encouraged to contact a health visitor at the health clinic or doctor's surgery, since a health visitor can often become a good, trusted friend:

> When my mother died I was left in the role of caring for my disabled father. The health visitor visited daily at first to make sure I was coping, and she made the arrangement for my father to enter a nursing home.

## Counsellor

In a growing number of primary health care teams, another important member is the counsellor. They are available to listen to the needs of carers, to be a safe place for carers to share their deepest fears, hurts and pains. They rarely go out to homes, but are based in the surgery, thus giving the carer an opportunity to get away from his situation, provided, of course, that someone else can sit with the dependant for that time.

## Hospital staff specialist

The GP may refer the dependant to a hospital consultant, a specialist in treatment of a particular condition or disease. Some hospital consultants are:

Geriatrician – who specialises in diseases of elderly people

Paediatrician – who specialises in care of children and childhood diseases

Neurologist – who specialises in diseases of the brain and nervous system

Orthopaedic Surgeon – who specialises in problems caused by diseases or injury of the bones

Psychiatrist – who specialises in mental illness or mental handicap in any age group

Psychogeriatrician – who specialises in mental illness in elderly people.

The normal pattern is for the GP to write a referral letter to a named consultant asking for an appointment for an out-patient clinic. Before this appointment, encourage carers to sit down and make a list of the important questions they want to ask. If carers are unable to transport themselves and their dependants it may be appropriate to offer to transport them to hospital.

If getting a dependant to hospital is completely out of the question, the GP can request a home visit where the consultant visits the patient in his or her own home, which can be far less harrowing for all. Of course some consultants are more helpful than others, but carers need to be encouraged to be specific with their questions and needs. A hospital consultant is able to assess a problem and advise on treatment, as well as organise:

A place in a day hospital for a dependant

A short stay in hospital, for assessment, treatment or respite care

Regular short stays in hospital

Permanent care in hospital or nursing home.

**The social worker**

The social worker is the 'open door' to many local authority services and may be able to organise:

Home help

Care attendant

Meals on wheels

Appropriate equipment for daily living

Adaptations to the dependant's home

Laundry service

Day centre or sheltered workshop for dependant

Respite care

Holidays

Long-term residential care

For young children, a place at a special school

Contact with local support groups.

Social workers are key workers in the help and support of carers. They have a legal duty to inform carers of local authority services, so the information they give will be up to date. They often know a lot about local voluntary and self-help groups and thus can help and advise on a wide range of practical, personal and financial problems. Some social services offer specialist social workers who cater to the particular needs of the elderly, those handicapped in their hearing or sight, the mentally ill, those physically and mentally handicapped, etc. It is worth while making a telephone call to social services to find out if they have a specialist social worker with experience suited to a particular situation. This is something anyone can do for busy carers.

## Physiotherapist

Physiotherapists are trained to care for dependants with mobility problems. Depending on the part of the country, there may be community physiotherapists attached to GP surgeries, or based in hospitals. Community physiotherapists make home visits to help improve the dependant's mobility and fitness, and for a child this may involve play therapy. If there is a need for a physiotherapist to visit, ask the GP if this can be arranged. A physiotherapist is usually in a position to organise and arrange for:

Walking aids, such as crutches, sticks and zimmer frame (walking frame)

A wheelchair if the dependant needs one regularly.

## Occupational therapist

The role of the occupational therapist is to visit handicapped people of all ages and to teach them how to manage ordinary everyday tasks, such as eating, washing, dressing and bathing, and to give advice.

Occupational therapists work in hospitals and in the community, occasionally under other titles such as 'Adviser to the Handicapped' or 'Rehabilitation Officer'. In the community they can be contacted through the local authority and are based in the social services department.

Occupational therapists also advise on what equipment or home adaptations might be of help and may be able to arrange:

Adaptations to the home, for example, installing a stair lift, fitting ramps, widening doors and installing a lavatory/shower downstairs

Equipment to help with everyday living, for example, commodes, wheelchairs, chairs with high seats, adapted cutlery, washing helps, dressing helps and handrails beside bath and/or lavatory.

## Speech therapist

A speech therapist is able to help adults or children with speech/language difficulties. Such difficulties often accompany a handicap, illness, stroke, or perhaps a head injury, as well as muscle-wasting diseases. Speech therapists are trained to work in all these areas. They generally work in schools and health clinics, occasionally making home visits. Ask the GP or health visitor for an appropriate referral.

## Chiropodist

Chiropodists are trained to take care of the feet – an essential service for the elderly or disabled. Unfortunately, free chiropody is scarce – even if a dependant is in the NHS priority group for free service (women over sixty, men over sixty-five, pregnant women, people who are mentally or physically handicapped). Chiropodists work in surgeries and health centres and hospitals, and also do home visiting. If the dependant needs special shoes or foot care, the GP can be asked to make an appointment with a chiropodist, or give the carer a contact number. Chiropodists are listed in *Yellow Pages*, and the local district health authority keeps a list, but make sure that the chosen chiropodist is state registered (SRCh).

## Dentist

If the dependant cannot visit the dentist, a home visit may be available. If the carer cannot find a visiting dentist, telephone the district health authority and ask for the district dental officer who will give the names of NHS dentists who make home visits. To find out if the dependant qualifies for free dental treatment, telephone Freefone Social Security on 0800 666555 or obtain the leaflet *Help with NHS Costs* by the DSS (AB 11).

## Optician

Again, the DSS leaflet *Help with NHS Costs* shows whether a dependant qualifies for vouchers towards the cost of glasses. Offer to help contact local opticians and ask whether they make free visits; if not, ascertain how much they charge. If you do not find an optician, contact the district health authority and ask for the local community health council, who may give information about visiting opticians.

## Home help/care assistant

Social services have a department responsible for sending help and care into the homes where needed. In different counties the people who give such help have different names; their jobs also vary considerably with different duties and responsibilities. Among other names they may be called home helps, home care assistants, care attendants, community care or domiciliary care. In some areas available personnel are home helps who offer a few hours each week to take responsibility for light jobs around the house such as cooking, cleaning and shopping; whereas in other areas home care assistants help with washing and dressing, preparing meals, shopping and occasionally housework. If help is available from the social services, no matter what the helper is called, carers ought to have a good idea of what she will or won't do from the beginning, as this can prevent bad feeling. It is important for carers as far as possible to find out from the home help organiser the times when help may be available and to work out a checklist of responsibilities.

Most local authorities will take a referral for help from anybody: GPs, neighbour, family member, and will require details such as the physical health of the dependant, medical information and a statement of need for that particular person. Usually social services make a home visit for assessment of the practical need and will also make a financial assessment. This is worked out according to the financial position of the dependant. Help cannot be given if the dependant does not want it, even if the carer does. Carers cannot therefore be in control of this help, unless the dependant is under age. Because of a huge demand for home helps in some areas, there may be a waiting list. To overcome this problem and to meet growing needs, private care attendance schemes are increasingly available (see *Yellow Pages* for addresses).

## Care attendant

There are many different schemes with different names, but broadly speaking they aim to provide help to fit the needs of carers and their dependants. This may include help with washing and dressing, jobs around the house or perhaps sitting with the dependant while the carer goes out. They try to be flexible enough to fill the gaps wherever needed. Depending on whether the scheme is voluntary or private there may be a small charge. Care attendants are normally trained, and carers would be well advised to clarify exactly how much training they have received and whether there are certain tasks they will not take responsibility for.

The Association of Crossroads Care Attendance Scheme (see Appendix 1 for address) has initiated a scheme as a model of support for carers offering practical help of whatever nature carers require – attendants are trained to undertake any task the carers themselves would perform, except the administration of drugs. Crossroads have over 100 schemes across the country and are often funded by local authorities.

Other schemes are:

Family Support Services

Neighbourhood Care Attendant Schemes

Extended Home Help Schemes

Home Care Attendant or Assistant Schemes

Cheshire Family Support Schemes.

Carers may be so restricted by the demands of caring that they are not aware that other members of the primary health care team apart from the GP, and other key workers, are able to help in numerous practical ways. We can help carers by identifying the key workers and their areas of responsibility so that we can point carers in the right direction for appropriate help in their individual circumstance.

# 11

# Practical Support

Caring is not a public activity – it goes on behind the closed doors of the individual's home. As we've already noted, carers often find it difficult to ask for practical help; they feel they are always taking and never in a position to give anything in return. Even if practical support is offered, carers are occasionally reluctant to accept it because they fear it will not be carried out in the way they would like, or that perhaps it will be unreliable. Carers may feel that there is a lot of enthusiasm to help them during an immediate crisis, but they naturally wonder whether people will still be there helping in one, two, three years' time. It is therefore essential that we who offer to help carers have thought fully about a realistic commitment in time and energy.

The needs of carers vary according to their relationship to the person for whom they are caring, so while many needs are universal, every carer will approach them in her or his own way. Hence we need to consult carers about what help they would like rather than giving them help we think essential. As we build friendships with carers, the division between needs and wants becomes clearer and our response more appropriate.

For those who care for relatives in their own homes the demands may be relentless. The day may start in the early hours with washing and dressing the dependant, and not end until the exhausted carer has put him to bed and turned out the light fourteen to fifteen hours later. To relieve the tedious day-to-day routine it is helpful to think of creative, practical ways to break the monotony. A surprise visit, for example, means a different face and personality filling the home – very refreshing for carers. A timely visit with a gift such as a bunch of flowers, fresh fruit, a box of chocolates or a favourite home-baked cake can speak volumes to carers, as these comments by Lynn show:

> My husband and I had just had a terrible row with my mother who was suffering with Alzheimer's disease. Our secretary, working in the home, was aware of this and the strain we were under, so she went out and bought some cream cakes for us, to cheer us along the way. It was such a little gesture, but said so much!

Look at the daily routine together and encourage carers to change their routine tasks where possible and become more creative in their approaches. Some carers, for example, may have become so 'locked in' to being the carer that they may not see that a granny who is crippled but still mentally alert, would probably love to read to the children. This could have several benefits. It would give the carer a few minutes' space, could improve relation-ships between Gran and the younger members of the household, and heighten Granny's self-esteem, making her less dependent emotionally on the carer.

Encourage carers, too, to consider the practical implications of having pets in the home. According to circumstances pets can be a nuisance or a great blessing, as Vera found out:

> My husband is immobile and sits in the chair most of the day. Our cat curls up and sleeps in his lap every morning. The cat's comforting presence with him releases me to get the chores done as my husband isn't as lonely or demanding when the cat is with him.

Providing basic practical help for carers means being a good neighbour. It requires that we offer some or all of the following:

To buy or collect anything they might need from the shops

To fetch a prescription from the chemist

To help mow the lawn or weed the garden

To undertake the DIY jobs around the house (ie, leaking taps)

To make an occasional meal

To bath the children

To take the children out for a day's outing

To be available at the other end of the telephone

To sit in with dependants occasionally, so the carer can have a special day out

To sit with a dependant and play games, read suitable literature, or talk about the past, etc.

These comments from carers show how important these things which are small to us can be:

I wanted to cry and say, 'Ask what favourite meal we would like. As my energy level isn't high enough to be creative, please cook us something.'

A kind neighbour offered to help with some of the ironing. It's hard for me to stand for long periods, so I found this offer of great benefit in spite of having to swallow my pride and receive help.

Having thought of ways to break up the daily routine, try to help the carer schedule 'withdrawal periods' into the weekly routine. Leisure, recreation, hobbies, sport, nights out with friends may have become a forgotten world; the carer loses all sense of her own identity. Offers to sit in with a dependant on a regular weekly basis allow carers to have space for themselves – space in which to go out and join clubs and organisations, etc. Sitters/relief carers need to offer plenty of time to carers giving them a wide margin either side of their time off. So often carers become people who rush everywhere, feeling that they must get back as soon as possible, which is not very good for the blood pressure and reduces the value of the outing. The respite care offered must be accessible, flexible and appropriate to the circumstances. It can make an amazing difference to someone, as Maud describes:

I looked forward to Tuesdays so much; it was the day a young sixth former (on community service from the local college) came and sat with my husband. It allowed me the freedom to get out of the house, have a breath of fresh air, go to the shops and have no demands for one afternoon a week.

If carers look after a relative in their own home they frequently say that what they would appreciate more than anything else is to have their home all to themselves for an afternoon. Where possible it may be helpful for the dependant to be taken out regularly, so that carers are able to enjoy their own homes in peace and quiet, as Charlotte experienced:

I found the most helpful support came from a group of friends who arranged a rota, inviting my elderly, confused mother out for a couple of hours on a weekly basis.

Another possible demonstration of practical love is suggested by the following remarks:

I knew I had a breather on Mondays, as a friend went in regularly to visit. The day was my own; I didn't have to fit visiting into my schedule and I didn't have to listen to my mother continually asking when she could go home. That day apart gave me strength and energy to cope with the rest of the weekly visits.

Besides receiving daily and/or weekly respite care, carers will almost certainly benefit from an occasional weekend or holiday away. Some carers, though, however well-earned the holiday, will find it difficult to relax because of their 'excess baggage' – the weight of anxiety for the relative left behind and guilty concern that the dependant may deteriorate in their absence.

The social services or GP may be able to arrange respite care to allow the carer to have a holiday or a weekend break, or alternatively the solution may be in voluntary help. As we saw with Jean Tame's story, the Christian organisation CARE (see Appendix 1 for address) organises the CARE Homes Programme which offers love and support to carers by welcoming them into Christian homes for a break. The duration of the stay rests with the hosts, but can be anything from a weekend to a fortnight, and occasionally a longer period is available. A local CARE co-ordinator is involved in arranging appropriate placements. Guests are required to make some financial contribution from either private or state funds. This is what Tim, a young man, had to say:

I enjoyed my stay with this family because I was surrounded by love. By accepting me they gave me a sense of self-worth and I realised through their practical demonstration of love how real God is and how much he cares for me. I returned home feeling more relaxed and ready to face the unknown by the guiding hand of God.

In some areas other schemes encourage local families to accept a handicapped person into their home for a weekend to give the carer a rest. This form of 'Adopt a Disabled Person' scheme not only enriches the life of the disabled person by giving him new experiences and friendships, but also gives carers a much needed break.

Alternatively, a friend actually staying in the

dependant's home for a weekend will give far more security and continuity, and carers (and perhaps families) are able to go away themselves for a break. The benefits of this are much appreciated as Shirley states:

> We have one friend, recently retired, who will come and stay for a week or a weekend, to allow my husband and me to be away together with our two teenage children. This is priceless! Placing Mum in the local old people's home for a fortnight last summer was a disaster.

Breaks for carers need to be started gradually and built up over a period of time so that the dependant can adjust to a new face and a different person caring. For example, the sitter/relief carer might, at first, just pop in for a cup of tea and slowly increase this time until the carer feels that a good enough friendship has been established to allow the relief carer to take over for a while. On the other hand, if a dependant is going to stay at a relief carer's home, perhaps for the first one or two visits the carer should go along too. It is very important to build confidence between the person being cared for and a sitter/relief carer.

After a break, carers would be advised to assess with the person they care for as well as the sitter/relief carer how the break went. Bear in mind that there is always a possibility of the dependant playing one carer off against another. Therefore it is vitally important that difficulties are discussed and changes made as necessary. The quality of the substitute care is extremely important, not only for the dependant, but also for the carer's peace of mind. If having a sitter/relief carer is not working out, then looking at different avenues might help.

If the carer's role is temporarily taken over because of holidays or illness, be aware of several factors. The routine and the likes and dislikes of the dependant, together with information such as medication, handling of incontinence, use of equipment, relevant telephone numbers, etc, should be passed on, preferably written down. Specifically, the sitter/relief carer must have some knowledge of the following:

## Medication

As some drugs can obviously be dangerous if taken incorrectly, medication alone can cause unnecessary worry, particularly if it has to be rigidly taken at a set time with the correct dosage. The dependant herself may be perfectly capable of handling her medicines, but in the carer's absence she may have to be given them. Never rely on instructions on the packet or bottle, but always ask the carer to write down the relevant information – the time and amount of tablets or medicine. Be aware that some drugs must not be combined with alcohol and be sure that you know any possible side-effects of the drugs. Some chemists sell plastic containers for pills with compartments labelled 'Monday, Tuesday, Wednesday' – especially useful to remind busy carers whether or not a pill has been given. The Disabled Living Foundation Information Service gives a list of suppliers from which these pill dispensers are available.

## Incontinence

'Urinary incontinence' refers to the lack of control of urine, while 'faecal incontinence' refers to a loss of bowel control. The two kinds of incontinence do not necessarily go together, but when they do a person is said to be doubly incontinent. Sometimes incontinence is more a question of an accident than loss of control, so it is important to try to take preventive steps.

Frequent visits to the toilet, and clothing which is easy to undo, will help. Equipment such as a raised toilet seat and/or a rail by the toilet may also help. A potty chair for a child, or a commode and/or urinal for an adult could reduce the stress of coping with accidents. There are many other ways to help the carer, as Christine describes:

I helped my mother sew velcro into many of my father's clothes, and this made such a difference. When he wanted to go to the toilet it was so much easier to open his trousers with velcro, rather than trying to find the zip end or undo buttons.

For most people, going to the toilet is a private and personal thing; tact, gentleness and understanding are called for. It is very important to be sensitive about this and to encourage the person being cared for to be as independent as possible. Ask them when they want to go to the toilet and how they like to manage it.

Accidents at night are common so it may be helpful to limit the amount of fluid consumed in the evening. Leaving a night light on throughout the night may help, and it is advisable to have a commode, urinal or potty seat in the bedroom near the bed. Occasionally it is helpful to wake the person regularly at the same time during the night. Visiting the toilet then can save an accident later. This can create a problem, however, for the carer. Here's how one family solved it:

> I had to get up several times in the middle of the night to help my father to the toilet. I got so tired; he would go back to sleep, but I wouldn't. The district nurse suggested we tried the use of a urinal. This has made such a difference as now I sleep through most nights. We have had the occasional accident with the urinal tipping up – but nothing I can't cope with.

If the bowel becomes blocked with hard, old faeces, diarrhoea may start as liquid waste matter seeps past the blockage. A mixed diet that includes plenty of fibre is important.

When looking after a dependant, the sitter/relief carer should know where to find the stock of incontinence pads and pants, etc. They should also know the carer's normal procedure for disposing of soiled garments and freshening the air in the room.

Although dealing with incontinence can be embarrassing and unpleasant, it is important that the relationship doesn't suffer because of wrong attitudes. Remember that who people are is more important than what they do. A practical, efficient approach helps, and it is good to try to maintain a sense of humour – laughing at situations is much better than getting angry or crying.

## Lifting

It is very easy unknowingly to put a strain on your back, as Clive discovered:

> I often think what life would be like if I was ever relieved of the task of caring for my mother – a pain-free back!

To acquire the art of lifting without injuring the back is vital. You do need to learn the correct way, particularly as you have to undertake many different manoeuvres in the process. The strength, mobility of the dependant and the degree to which he is able to co-operate will affect the lifting and manoeuvring. However, some basic rules for lifting ought also to be kept in mind:

Bend at the knees and/or hips (the back must always be kept straight)

Tightening the stomach and thigh muscles on lifting will lessen back strain

Keep your feet apart to form a firm base from which to lift

Avoid twisting your back as you lift

Be particularly careful when in a hurry or weary.

If the dependant falls, and is too heavy to be lifted, get help by calling an ambulance, or request the help of a strong neighbour.

## Difficult behaviour

Unusual or unacceptable behaviour by the person being cared for may seem to be deliberate, particularly if the role of caring has been taken over by a relief carer. Find out from carers the ways in which the person being cared for may behave and how to respond. Whatever happens, remain calm: irritation, nervousness or even panic can be infectious. Responses should be given in a slow, quiet voice (provided the dependant is not deaf!). Trying to sense what the dependant is feeling will bring greater understanding than trying to rationalise what she is doing. If the dependant feels lost, confused or uncertain about what is happening she is more likely to respond in a distressing or annoying manner. Having someone else in the caring role may completely confuse a dependant, so try to be as reassuring as possible and explain what is going on, and what is going to happen. Keeping to the same daily pattern can bring a sense of security while the dependant's carer is away.

Sometimes the person being cared for wanders off or behaves in a bizarre way in public. Sympathetic neighbours may help, and the local police may also be understanding. Practical measures like locking doors and gates will prevent dependants strolling away, and they should always carry some form of personal identification:

Their pension card

A letter with their address

Identity bracelet with address and telephone number.

## Problems with communication

Communicating with someone is more than just talking. Facial expressions and touching can speak volumes. Speak simply and clearly about one topic at a time – offer one choice at a time. For example, asking an elderly person who will probably have some degree of hearing loss if he wants to watch the news may be confusing, but if you stand by the television – which is a visual clue – and say, 'It's time for the news on television. Would you like to watch it?' they will pick up the visual clue that you are standing by the television and pointing to it and the word 'television' gives them a clue about the kind of question you are going to ask next. Giving plenty of time to respond is essential; if someone is rushed he may become confused or aggressive. If communication is difficult using simple sign language, mime or the use of picture cards may be helpful.

Playing the guessing game can make the frustration worse. If the dependant is unable to feed himself, frustration can arise because the relief carer is not sure about the speed at which the person can eat food. Guessing that they want more food may cause choking! Discussing small things like this beforehand with the regular carer can avoid a lot of problems.

Although verbal abuse is distressing, little can be done, and it is better to ignore it. Even if there is very little response from the dependant, just being alongside, communicating through relaxed conversation with signs of affection, reassures him that someone cares enough to give him attention.

Every carer's needs are different. Innovative and imaginative offers of practical help with real regard to the particular circumstances of the carer will bring welcome respite from the continuous role of caring.

To sum up: ask yourself (and God) what *you* can

do to help a carer. Before impulsively offering, think it through carefully – can you realistically offer long-term help on a regular basis? What are your gifts? Don't offer to make a meal every week if you hate cooking. Take into account the carer's needs and desires. Would she like you to bathe the children, or would she prefer you to sit with Grandad so that, for once, she can enjoy an unhurried bath-time with them? Would she rather get out and do the shopping by herself, or have you do it?

If you volunteer respite care, take time to get to know the dependant and establish a good relationship. Make sure you have written down all the information you might need. Be prepared to adapt your speech and mannerisms accordingly. Although you may feel you haven't much to offer, giving where and as you can will undoubtedly bless the carer beyond anything you can imagine.

# 12

# *Emotional Support*

As caring always takes place in the context of a relationship, it brings with it a vast range of feelings, from utter despair to deep joy. Carers may feel at times that their emotions are out of control, as they are interwoven with those of the person being cared for, as well as with circumstances, both of which carers have little power to control. Pat wept for the first time as she shared these words:

> Nobody knows what it is really like. On the outside I appear to manage, but on the inside I am in pieces. People haven't the least idea what I am feeling. I pretend that I am fine – if only people knew what I was really feeling like.

The Christian church has a ministry to the whole person. It recognises that carers have needs beyond the practical – inner needs for love and friendship. Some churches have a 'listeners' group which offers people a listening ear; whereas other churches encourage and train their members to nurture skills required to walk alongside those who feel lonely and isolated. The church, as Christ's body on earth, has a unique role to play in caring for the carers by demonstrating how much God values and cares for those who are oppressed and heavy laden.

The most valuable support any carer can be given is the recognition that she is unique and that how she feels is of concern and importance. Encourage her to take off the protective mask at least long enough to let her real feelings be known to you. She can only feel accepted when she is genuinely and attentively listened to. Listening means concentrating on the words and the underlying feelings that someone is expressing, rather than mentally rehearsing a suitable response. Kathy longed for a listening ear:

> When coming to terms with my child's handicap, I needed more help in terms of people coming round to visit me, to weep with me and to listen (for more than ten seconds).

Carers can develop such a tunnel vision that things get out of perspective. By listening to small yet significant problems, as well as larger ones, we can help carers to see the situation more objectively and to put things into perspective. Conveying love and support for carers will sometimes involve listening to the retelling of details of the loved one's handicap, illness or disability. Carers can thus ventilate their feelings and come to terms with the present.

Feelings are neither right nor wrong; they are part of our humanity. Everyone reacts differently to a situation. Feelings are personal and the mechanism adopted to cope with feelings will be unique for every individual. Therefore carers need to be able to share *how* they feel, with no sense of judgement or disgust from the listener – as Kathy experienced:

> My GP was the only person (other than my husband) who listened consistently to how I felt, and who didn't expect anything from me.

Allow carers to be honest about their feelings, their concerns, their limitations and their behaviour. Accept carers *where* they are and *how* they are. Don't try to put pressure on them to be anyone else other than who they are – let them be unique persons with their own feelings. Let carers know that it is completely acceptable to feel emotion, and that they will be supported through the pain. Reassure them that they are not bad if they experience negative emotions; it is what they do with them that matters. What one carer can cope with will drive another to the brink of despair. Andrea found moments of despair in her caring:

> I have all these feelings bottled up inside … very few people understand. But those who do, are like gold as I can off-load onto them my feelings of anger, resentment and at times hate – yet I love my father really.

As well as listening, empathising is healing, as we tune in to carers' feelings and encourage them to dig a little deeper, to allow the pain to surface and be acknowledged. When these feelings are accepted without judgement, shock or embarrassment, carers are released from remorse and self-blame and thus helped along the road to handling their emotions. As Fiona expressed:

> The most helpful friend was the one who cried *with* me. Some people are afraid to cry with someone in case it makes them worse. It is actually very healing to 'weep with those who weep'.

It may be helpful to encourage carers to talk about their feelings by asking them such questions as: 'What do you resent about the situation?'; 'What are the good things?'; 'How do you feel?'; 'How are you coping?'

> I never allowed myself to feel – that is until a friend came alongside me and encouraged me to talk. At first I felt frightened with realising the turmoil that was going on inside me. The more I talked, slowly this improved. I am so grateful for my friend who listened and asked me the occasional question.

Great patience and energy may be called for as we listen to carers who share their raw pain. A carer's response to her situation may be irrational anger targeted at friends or family, but a lack of resentment or annoyance in return is always constructive.

All carers go through some measure of emotional upheaval. Identifying and coping with the emotions listed here will certainly help carers.

## Anger

Anger can grow from irritation, disappointment, frustration, hurt and resentment, all of which may lead to a deep bitterness, but in the end achieve nothing except to make it more difficult for carers to work in the way they want to. Accordingly, it is useful to help carers identify what they actually resent. Is it what they have to do? Or what they are prevented from doing. Or do they resent God, or the person they are caring for? Wherever possible, help carers to tackle the root of these feelings. Vera found it difficult to have a break because her husband wouldn't let her, and said:

> I feel very bitter that I have lost my freedom in having to care for my husband.

Helping carers to come to the place of letting go of resentment and forgiving people where necessary, is an important part of caring for them. Of course they may feel resentful at times, but it is the letting go of the resentment that is important:

> See to it that no-one misses the grace of God and that no bitter root grows up to cause trouble and defile many (Heb 12:15).

Anger is an understandable and normal feeling, but it often brings guilt – many people find anger the most unacceptable of feelings. Yet not all anger is sinful. The Bible instructs us: 'In your anger do not sin' (Eph 4:26). It is entirely feasible to be angry without sinning: there is a distinction between the strong emotion we call anger and the seething hostility that can be an inappropriate expression of it. Unresolved anger motivates us to hurt others, to inflict pain on someone unconnected with the root of the anger. Carers may take the anger out on their families.

Once they accept that feeling angry is not wrong or inappropriate they may need help to express their anger appropriately. These steps may help:

Acknowledge the anger. If it is repressed it is buried alive and it will do damage. It may be hard to be honest about the feeling, but God can only meet people at the place of honesty.

Confess it to God. He is big enough and always loving enough to cope with anger and he will help people to deal with it.

Express it appropriately, ie, don't lose self-control or let it lead into sin.

Mary said:

I feel so angry that he takes me for granted – he never says thank you. This turns into resentment and I know that I don't do anything out of love any more.

There are other ways in which we can resolve anger:

By making the root cause a matter of prayer

By a spirit of love and forgiveness

By realising that no offence by anybody could possibly equal our own guilt before God. Yet in his mercy he has forgiven mankind and therefore expects the same attitude of mercy and forgiveness to others.

Anger and unforgiveness can be very destructive. This is how Doreen dealt with it:

I get so angry and frustrated with her – I want to lash out. The only way I can cope is to walk out of the room, and shut myself away with some beautiful worship songs playing. Then, having calmed down and realised again just how loving God is to me, I can go back and be loving to my daughter.

All anger produces biochemical changes in the body and it is important that carers have opportunities to expend some of this energy, maybe through:

Playing a sport, eg, badminton

Going for walks

Being creative

Organising a support group

Relaxing and finding activities that bring fun and enjoyment.

## Guilt

Many carers say guilt is the strongest of all their feelings because however much they do for their dependants, they feel it is not enough. Help carers to identify what they feel guilty about. For example, they may be 'caring' out of guilt, trying to make up in some way for something in the past. Feeling guilty makes it very difficult for carers to receive help as they feel they ought to be coping and that they have failed in their duty if they ask for help. Robert said:

When I went out to the shops I was always asked, 'When will you be back? You won't forget me, will you?' Then if I stayed out longer than we had established, I felt guilty that I had let my wife down, and angry that I had lost my freedom.

How can carers make sense of their feelings of guilt? We need to help them separate destructive self-condemnation from the genuine convicting of the Holy Spirit. Feeling guilty about something that is wrong can act as the final signal of recognition of sin, which in turn can lead to repentance. However, carers very often carry guilt even when they haven't done anything wrong. We need to help carers see the difference between true and false guilt. True guilt – convicting by the Holy Spirit – is usually specific and something can be done about it: confess, repent, forget. False guilt is vague, general, non-specific, and nothing can be done to alter anything anyway.

## Depression

Most carers are 'low' at some time or other, and these patches range from very mild (feeling low for a few hours) to very severe (feeling hopeless and discouraged for days, weeks or months on end). In the black pit of depression carers may suffer feelings of inadequacy, anxiety, worthlessness, panic attacks, overwhelming tiredness and utter hope-lessness, having lost all hope for the future. With these feelings come physical aches and pains.

For many carers, high expectations of fulfilment and satisfaction in marriage, family life and a job do not materialise. This discrepancy between hope and reality, the 'should and ought' and the 'what if?', often leads to depression. The greater the discrepancy between hope and non-fulfilment, the greater the potential for depression. Jane knew this feeling:

I don't want to wake up in the morning. I just want to lie in bed all day. Then I won't have to face the pain of the situation.

Unrealistic expectations can also arise from a faulty self-image. Rather than accepting themselves as they are, for who they are, carers are often driven by an inner voice saying, 'I should do better. I should be able to manage.' We can help carers to see that they don't have to be super-saints in the way they give care – always striving for an impossible standard of perfect caring. We need to talk through with carers whether their expectations of themselves and their situations are unrealistically high or truly from the Lord. If their goals are unrealistic, every day will be full of disappointment, leading in turn to anger and depression. Encourage carers to see who they are in Christ – 'There is now no condemnation for those who are in Christ Jesus' (Rom 8:1) – and to set more realistic goals.

Another major contributor to depression is self-pity. Although for carers this is understandable, it can nevertheless be a destructive emotion and a doorway to depression. Encourage carers to be on the alert for any thoughts that could be concluded with, 'Poor old me,' or, 'I am a helpless victim in this situation.' Remind carers that God himself is caring for them, encouraging them to look at the positive things in their situation and to make the best of these. Both will help carers fight the tendency to self-pity.

I've discovered a fighting spirit within me – and the chief enemy is self-pity. I abhor it in my dependent mother, when really her life has been very easy and I am determined not to give way to it myself.

But sometimes talking is not enough and some carers may need medical help from their GP. Anti-depressant or tranquillising drugs may seem to offer an instant solution. Equally, they may become habit-forming, and they don't change the circumstances. Finding a way of coping within the circumstances is the best help that can be offered to carers, as no drug can substitute for working through the problem and finding the best solution.

## Grief and loss

Grief can arise from seeing a person changed by illness or age, or from mourning the loss of the person who might have been. Helping carers to face that loss will be a healing work. In some situations, there may be an added dimension to their grieving: to see a loved one suffering in pain, with very often a changing personality and loss of dignity, may make carers very vulnerable to the growing pressures for euthanasia. It is very understandable for carers to want to bring an end to the suffering – not only the dependant's suffering but theirs also. It is here that Christians need both to reach out with sacrificial love to support carers in their pain and anguish, and to stand firm on their belief in the sanctity of life. Human life is God's gift to us; every human life is uniquely precious and it is God's responsibility alone to decide when our earthly life should finish. At present, euthanasia is not a legal option in this country, but there is an increasing demand that it should become so.

Helping carers to acknowledge and talk about their grief is essential. Grieving is different for everyone, so just standing alongside someone grieving gives great support. Occasionally there is more grieving before death than afterwards, particularly if a dependant has Alzheimer's Disease, as there is a loss of love, recognition, relationship and partnership, even though the person is still there in the physical sense. So grief is often present, but it may be suppressed. Death can actually come as a relief in some cases, as David describes:

> I did all my crying before she died – I haven't got any tears left.

The death of a dependant can, however, bring the most difficult emotional strain for carers. They have not only suffered the loss of the person they knew, but they also face the traumatic loss of their caring role; one that has perhaps been a consuming full-time work, defining almost their whole existence. They therefore feel they have lost all their identity.

Grieving then affects the carers emotionally. It can also affect them physically. Extreme tiredness, muscular pain, heart palpitations, loss of appetite, dry mouth, damp hands and insomnia are just a few possible physical symptoms. Acute sadness may come in waves, and many tears will fall before the grief diminishes. Some carers may need permission to cry as Sue requested:

> Tell me it's OK to be sad and to be real with you, so that I'm free to cry if I want to.

The more carers allow themselves to cry the easier it will be for them to progress through the mourning process. Sue went on to say:

I didn't know it was possible to feel such sadness. It is almost like a physical pain.

Obviously, grief has to show up somewhere; suppressing it can cause a choking sensation, irregular breathing and weight loss. If carers find it difficult to talk about their feelings, then writing them in a journal or a poem can also release the pain of grief. Carers will need encouragement and support as they face the future adjusting to a different lifestyle; one for which they have probably longed, but for which they are nevertheless ill-equipped. If further help is needed in the grieving process, then CRUSE Bereavement Care offer voluntary help (see Appendix 1 for address).

## Loneliness

Some carers are lonely; they are isolated and rarely see or communicate with other people. Others may feel lonely in spite of being surrounded by many people; they feel no one really understands. Loneliness sharpens the depression, stress and guilt – there may seem no way out. Often, too, carers begin to lose confidence in themselves and are not able to step out and bridge the gap between themselves and the outside world. On the other hand, carers may be too embarrassed to invite people into their homes if those they care for behave oddly, are incontinent, or need constant attention. As far as possible, make daily contact with carers, particularly if they are susceptible to depression and loneliness, and try to persist with friendships, especially if carers are in difficulties. Remember that isolation from others is a common, very painful, experience for carers. Peter shares:

We really found who our close friends were, as only those who really cared bothered to pop in and see how we were. I felt hurt and rejected by those friends who dropped us because of my wife's illness, and I began to feel so lonely. In the end I had no energy or incentive to contact people. If only they had phoned me.

## Blessings

With the pain, some carers do experience positive feelings, and acknowledging and talking about them can be helpful, as Julia describes:

> I look after my mother who is suffering from Alzheimer's Disease and have made a list of blessings to my life:

> I have more time available for my children since I gave up my job for my mother.

> I see value and pleasure in things I previously took for granted.

> I'm learning patience, and how to be real and cry more easily.

> I have a greater sense of the Lord's presence – I've needed him!

Carers may find that blessings very often come through what seem to be losses. The pain of suffering and loss can somehow highlight the beauty and gains in life. Caring for a dependant may provide that precious commodity of time to establish a deeper relationship than perhaps would have been possible if circumstances were different:

> I have found a deeper contentment and peace than I have ever experienced before. In spite of losing my independence I have found a new depth within me. I wouldn't change places with anyone.

Children with special needs can be a great blessing to parents, as they are often warm and fun-loving in their own way. They can bring much joy into the home. Claire, a mother of a teenage daughter with special needs, has found this to be true:

> When Joanna was first born the Lord gave me the verse in Jeremiah 33:3 (RSV), 'Call unto me and I will show you great and mighty things that you know not.' My husband and I look back over the last eighteen years and can say a hearty 'Amen' to that promise. Today, Joanna is a lovely young lady, with Jesus very much in the centre of her life. It has been good to see her progress, but to have received so much ourselves from Joanna has also been a blessing.

Blessings may also be found in the privilege of caring for dying relatives where they are loved and nursed with dignity in their own home. For it is in giving that we receive. One carer, Alan, said:

> I find it a great pleasure to look after my dying wife and I wouldn't have it any other way. She is so grateful for everything I do, never grumbles, and always says 'thank you'. I thank God that she is such a blessing to me.

A culture that has no natural place for carers means more than ever that love and concern for carers should give them a sense of value, just as every individual is of value to God. May we be a channel of blessing to carers as we listen to them and support them in their emotional turmoil.

# 13

## *Spiritual Support*

The support of the local church and fellow Christians is vitally important for carers. When a dependant is no longer able to attend services owing to inappropriate behaviour, incontinence, or the inability to sit still, carers nearly always stop going, too. As carers are often invisible on Sundays it is easy to forget them, but their need may be even greater in this enforced absence from Christian fellowship.

A group of people in the church or house group could get together and work out a weekly rota which would offer a sitter or relief carer for a Sunday service. The rota could also be extended to include mid-week meetings so that carers do not become too isolated from outside activities.

Regular prayer for carers and their own needs is as important as praying for the people they care for. It may be that close friends could make a regular commitment to pray for the carer and to keep themselves informed about current needs. Maybe once a week someone could go and pray with the carer for a few minutes.

Pastoral visits by ministers/elders can be of great support and if carers are not able to get to church, an offer to receive Holy Communion in their home may be welcome. Depending on the relationship, carers and dependants can take Holy Communion together or receive it separately; the Eucharist can bring a deep sense of comfort and reassurance that God is there in the situation with them. Sarah, a carer, testifies to the help given in this way:

> The vicar was of tremendous help at the beginning. While we were all trying to adjust to the shock of nursing a very ill father, he would visit and listen and pray with us. He helped us to keep our eyes upon Jesus.

Sometimes, the good intentions of church leaders and members can cause a great deal of hurt and distress. Help is often offered with the best of intentions, but without sensitivity – as Ray and Molly shared:

> The vicar saying, 'Why don't you put her in a home?' was very unhelpful to my husband and me. We are both in our sixties, caring for my ninety-six-year-old mother, and we found this advice very upsetting, as we want to care for her at home – but in doing that we are worn out. I used to be a church warden and I have been hurt by church members as they have wrongly assumed that because I spend time caring for my elderly relative I must have 'cooled' spiritually because I cannot attend church very often or get involved in the work. This attitude has caused me considerable pain.

Just as carers often find it difficult to ask for practical help, so they may also find it difficult to ask for spiritual help. Offering to pray with carers may be helpful, but we need to take care not to be super-spiritual – as John perceived:

> I felt that people were praying, but not understanding the depth of grief I was feeling and how long it took to adjust.

It is easy to heap coals of fire on the carers' pain by throwing out glib words that God will heal, when he hasn't specifically said that he will heal in a certain way. Carers are so vulnerable that they easily fall victim to guilt if they are asked, 'Haven't you prayed for their healing?' or, 'Where is your faith? God can do anything. Are you trusting?' Trying to rationalise the carers' pain by saying that God is in control (he is, but it needs to be said at the right moment when carers are ready to hear it) can cause greater pain than caring itself, as Barbara experienced:

> When I once explained that my son was and always would be doubly incontinent, someone said to me, 'Oh, that's all right, God will heal him.' I could have screamed at her. How dare she remind me of a God who I felt had already let me down?

It's difficult to go on offering meaning and hope to carers, but small gestures of loving concern may bring comfort and remind them that there is a God who loves them. Sending or giving carers a suitable card may be a small way of saying, 'I care about you.' It can, however, be a cop-out if it is not backed up with other forms of help and concern. Many cards give the message, 'I am thinking of you,' or, 'You are in my thoughts,' or quote an appropriate Bible verse. Perhaps a Christian book of daily readings, or a special picture, may speak volumes about how valued the carers are. If carers live at a distance, an occasional telephone call or letter to keep in touch may be an encouragement. Val emphasises the importance of scriptural promises:

Matthew 11:28–30 was very precious to me at the beginning and I still throw it at the Lord when things are bad. We find burdens heavy because (a) we don't share them, and (b) we take the person we care for too seriously.

'Come to me, all you who are weary and burdened, and I will give you rest. Take my yoke upon you and learn from me, for I am gentle and humble in heart, and you will find rest for your souls. For my yoke is easy and my burden is light.'

Help carers to realise that God does not remove every loss, hurt or difficulty, but he can work through them – turning each into a gain. God can take what seems to be a loss and through it give something better. This anonymous poem, believed to have been found on the body of a soldier, may be helpful.

*Gaining through Losing*

I asked God for strength, that I might achieve,
I was made weak, that I might learn humbly to obey.
I asked for health, that I might do greater things,
I was given infirmity, that I might do better things.
I asked for riches, that I might be happy,
I was given poverty, that I might be wise.

I asked for power, that I might have the praise of
  men,
I was given weakness, that I might feel the need of
  God.
I asked for all things, that I might enjoy life,
I was given life, that I might enjoy all things.
I got nothing that I asked for – but everything I had
  hoped for.
Almost, despite myself, my unspoken prayers were
  answered.
I am, among all men, most richly blessed.

Carers married to partners who have Alzheimer's
Disease, or who for other reasons have a personality change, are often painfully challenged by their
marriage vows, particularly the promise to love
and cherish in sickness and in health 'until death
us do part'. Looking after a partner who is unable
to recognise his wife, and has lost all recognition of
where he is, can be deeply distressing. Carers are
in turmoil and conflict. On the one hand they want
to keep their marriage vows, caring 'in sickness' as
well as 'in health', yet on the other they may be at
the end of their tether, defeated in their desire to
continue caring for their partners. At such time
carers are often helped by prayer to reach the right
decision as they discuss the situation with other
Christians and church leaders. Whatever they
decide, they will certainly need the support and
encouragement of friends in carrying the decision
through.

As we've already noted, carers often struggle
spiritually with the burden of guilt, and it is helpful
to talk with them about the difference between true
and false guilt. True guilt is when the Holy Spirit
convicts a person of wrong actions, thoughts or

words. It is like the red light on the car dashboard that signals something is wrong. If repentance, confession of the sin and a returning to God all follow, then the guilt has functioned as God intended. However, some guilt stems from an over-sensitive or scrupulous conscience. This is false guilt. Carers are often hyper-aware of every failure in their care for the dependants. Encourage them to accept their limitations, to see that everyone fails at times, and to believe the truth that they are precious to God, not because of what they do or fail to do, but because of who they are – precious and honoured in God's sight (Is 43:4).

The Soviet concentration camp survivor, Alexander Solzhenitzyn, said these words: 'All that the downtrodden can do is go on hoping. After every disappointment they must find fresh reason for hope.' The only really long-lasting hope that can be offered to carers is the hope there is in Jesus Christ. The book of Lamentations says:

One thing keeps me going –
this is what gives me hope –
I am still alive,
God's sympathy and understanding love keep
    coming to me.
They are new every morning. He never fails.
That's why I've chosen God.
I'll wait for him (Lam 3:19–24, author's own
    rendering).

# 14

## Support Groups

Many carers not only value the help and support of family, friends and neighbours, but also gain from voluntary and community schemes and groups. These non-profit-making organisations are usually run by volunteers and in some areas are supported with extra funding by the local health authority. Depending on local schemes, they may offer some of these and other services:

Organising and running support groups for carers to meet other people in similar circumstances

Providing extra services such as sitters, care attendants (either free or at a low cost), transport, equipment, a toy loan scheme, etc

Visiting and supporting carers at home

Representing the interests of carers and their dependants when local health and social services are being planned.

Information about such local voluntary and community schemes and groups should be available from a central office (in most areas) which is able to give details of local amenities. According to the area, the office may be called a Council for Voluntary Service, Voluntary Service Council, Voluntary Action Group, or a Rural Community Council. Their addresses and telephone numbers may be found in *Yellow Pages* under 'Charitable and Benevolent Organisations', or in an ordinary phone book. Failing this, contact the National Council for Voluntary Organisations (see Appendix 1 for address).

As already mentioned, CARE Trust supports carers with its CARE Homes programme. One of the Trust's stated aims is to encourage Christians in practical caring for their neighbours and it does this in a variety of ways. For example, it has available Bible study booklets on caring, and arranges conferences such as 'Caring for the Terminally Ill'.

Other sources of help are as follows: national organisations such as the Carers' National Association, the King's Fund Carers' Unit, Help the Aged and Age Concern, MIND and MENCAP (see Appendix 1 for addresses, plus other organisations); the Citizens Advice Bureau, Public Library or Town Hall; local social services department and social worker; the GP, district nurse, health visitor or hospital consultant. Meanwhile, a volunteer bureau or centre can give information about individual volunteers and the services they are able to offer, depending on the type of help requested. The centre may be listed in the phone book under 'Volunteer Bureau/Centre', etc or in the *Thomson Local Directory* under 'Charities and Voluntary Organisations'. The Volunteer Information Centre may also be able to help (see Appendix 1 for address).

A DIAL (Disablement Information and Advice

Line) exists in some areas, and the phone number can be found in the *Thomson Local Directory* under 'Help Lines' or in *Yellow Pages* under 'Disabled'. As all carers have different needs, they will expect different things from groups, and shopping around by visiting different groups will reveal what is available.

Carers often feel that those around them do not really understand the problems they face, and so benefit tremendously from contact with people who share and understand their situation. Groups exist for people coping with the same illness or disability, as well as for those caring in any capacity. In such groups they are able to share experiences, advice and information. In addition, many organisations produce useful and up-to-date publications and leaflets about dealing with particular problems, and these can be discussed in a group, as Shirley experienced:

> I meet monthly with other people caring for those with Alzheimer's Disease, and have found it very encouraging to share experiences and feelings and to know that other carers are human too!

## Women's groups

Some carers may want social contacts beyond the limited circle of carers and many women look for support from a group where they can relax and share their problems and feelings with other women. In some areas drop-in centres are open for women to go in for advice, information and a chat. The local community health council or Council for Voluntary Service will be able to advise if there is a group in the vicinity. The National Women's

Register (see Appendix 1 for address) is a non-political organisation which meets throughout the country and gives women the opportunity to listen to topical talks, have discussion groups and talk with other women. Alison found this particularly helpful:

> I really enjoy going to meet with other women. We are on the same wavelength, and this has helped me far more than any medicine.

## Social clubs

Social clubs also give opportunities to carers to get away from their day-to-day responsibilities and be involved in something completely different. All offer different opportunities: Rotary and Lion's Clubs, Townswomen's Guilds, Women's Institutes, etc. Charles enjoyed this diversion:

> I went off regularly to the Rotary Club and threw myself into its activities – it was wonderful to do something different and get away from the demands of caring for someone with dementia.

## Church groups

Ideally, for Christians, the church will be the strongest social group giving support. The church can build bridges between carers and people offering help and support by centralising all information about needs and available support. A large church could appoint someone to take responsibility for co-ordinating offers of help and carers' needs. Ideally this person should have experience of caring or health or social work. If resources allow, an information sheet regularly updated could help the local community as well as the church. The Jubilee Centre (see Appendix 1 for address) offers handbooks and videos on caring. The King's Fund produce *Caring at Home: A handbook for people looking after someone at home* (see Appendix 1 for address). Some churches are also beginning to organise information libraries and offer practical sessions on nursing skills, available equipment, communication, lifting, incontinence, dietary advice, etc. Jill has experienced the support of her local church and says:

My friends at church have been really helpful. After my husband was diagnosed as having only months to live, they organised a rota of people to come and sit with him, and another person would take me out for a meal.

However, sometimes it is difficult to find the support in the church that is hoped for, as this couple described:

Our son is with us twenty-four hours a day. He is nineteen years old, yet doesn't fit in with the teens at church, nor the children's work. We long to find ways of helping him to make friends – maybe this is just a dream. If he only had a group which he could identify with, and go out socially, not only would he benefit, but so would my husband and I. We would be free for that period of time to do together something we wanted. Although we have got so much to be thankful for in the love and support of our church, we feel let down that socially there is nothing for him.

## Self-help support groups

A self-help support group is a lifeline to many – it gives them a safe place where they can be honest about how they feel without fear of disapproval or misunderstanding, as Caroline experienced:

I feel so at home and comfortable in the group. For the first time I am able to share myself and am beginning to laugh about myself as I face concerns and worries, and realise that they can easily grow out of all proportion.

As well as being able to share information on the benefits and services available, these groups often arrange for special speakers and demonstrations for making caring easier. Whenever carers share deep hurts and needs, friendships develop. Carers then have friends they can turn to in a time of need, or for social times outside a meeting: 'I have found good friends in my carers' group and although talking about my problems doesn't make them go away, it certainly helps. I feel very accepted and valued – it is one time when I can lay aside my label as a carer and just be myself.'

If there is no appropriate local group, carers may appreciate encouragement to set up a local self-help group themselves. Identify the group's aims – are they social, supportive, self-help, informative, or to raise awareness in the community and campaigning for better services for carers? To contact interested people, a letter in the local paper, or an advert in a doctor's waiting room, a day centre or library, may identify other carers. At the outset, the group needs to think about where it will meet and how often, and how long the actual meetings will last. The comfort of the meeting place is important whether it is a home, church hall, or community centre. Other questions that need consideration are:

How accessible is the room? Is there a flight of stairs or a lift?

How will people get to and from the meeting? Is there a car park? What about public transport? Is it on a bus route? Will transport have to be provided?

Where will the finance to hire a hall come from?

Are there facilities to make coffee and tea?

Perhaps it will be possible to appoint a group of volunteers to sit in with dependants while carers attend the self-help group. Further advice can be sought from:

The Carers' National Association (see Appendix 1 for address), which produces leaflets advising how to set up a carers' support group, plus information such as membership, facilities and ideas for content of meetings

*Self-help Groups – Getting Started, Keeping Going* by Judy Wilson can be bought from bookshops (see Appendix 2)

*Setting up for Self-Help* is written by Contact a Family (see Appendix 1 for address). This is for people interested in setting up self-help groups for children with special needs and their families.

Support and help may be forthcoming from sources other than a formal group. We need to encourage carers to be creative in finding ways of support. One lady caring for her mother describes her solution:

> One thing that works well for me is to go out in a foursome with a couple where the husband has also had a stroke. He and mum commiserate about old age and strokes, while his wife and I talk about caring, and give each other mutual support.

## A last word

The needs of carers are numerous and varied. If Jesus were here in person today he would minister to them with love and compassion, being aware of their deep emotional and spiritual needs. He would walk alongside them, identifying with their hurts and pains. The same Jesus who ministered in Galilee 2000 years ago asks us to be available today to allow his Holy Spirit to bring love, comfort and support to the forgotten people – the carers.

Let the final word be with a carer called Vera, who reminds us of the urgent need.

> I am a carer for my husband who is seventy years old. I am seventy-three. My husband is fading away with Motor Neurone Disease. He has no strength in his upper body, so can't use his hands. I have to feed him, take him to the toilet, blow his nose, help him to get comfortable in a chair, turn him over in the middle of the night, wash, shave, bath and dress him. I can't leave him more than one hour, and if I am late, he asks me where I have been in an accusing way, as if I don't care about him. He has changed from being a kind, considerate, undemanding partner to being a withdrawn, bitter, demanding man. Whatever I do receives little thanks. A district nurse comes in to

bathe him twice a week, and he goes to a special Day Unit two afternoons a week. There is no way out. As I look ahead, I see he will only deteriorate. I am at the end of my tether. I can't cope much longer, yet he refuses to go into a home; he pleads with me not to put him in one. I can't hold out much longer. I am exhausted. I need caring for ... I need help.

This lady – the author's mother – died very suddenly with a stroke – a wonderful way for her out of an impossible situation. At times she experienced loneliness and a sense that life was passing her by; at other times she felt encouraged, supported and cared for. We have an obligation to share the neighbour-love of Jesus Christ, and this can be expressed in caring for the carers.

# PART 3

## *Useful Information*

# APPENDIX 1

## *Useful Addresses*

*Inclusion in this list does not necessarily imply endorsement by the author or by CARE, of an organisation in every aspect of its work.*

**ACET (AIDS Care, Education and Training)** PO Box 1323, London W5 5TF (081–840 7879).

**Advisory Centre for Education** 18 Victoria Park Square, London E2 9PB (Tel: 081–980 4596).

**Age Concern** Bernard Sunley House, 60 Pitcairn Road, Mitcham, Surrey CR4 3LL (Tel: 081–640 5431).

**Alzheimer's Disease** 158–160 Balham High Road, London SW12 9BM (Tel: 081–675 6557). For carers of people with any form of dementia.

**Assistance and Independence for Disabled People Vehicle Supplies (Aid Vehicles Supplies)** Hockley Industrial Centre, Hooley Lane, PO Box 26, Redhill, Surrey RH1 6JF (Tel: 0737 770030).

**ARC (Association for Residential Care)** The Old Rectory, Church Lane North, Old Wittington, Chesterfield S41 9QY (Tel: 0246 455881).

**Association of Continence Advisers** Disabled Living Foundation, 380–384 Harrow Road, London W9 2HU (Tel: 071–289 6111).

**Association of Crossroads Care Attendance Schemes** 10

Regent Place, Rugby, Warwickshire CV21 2PN (Tel: 0788 573 653).

**Association for the Pastoral Care of the Mentally Ill** 39 St John's Lane, London EC1M 4BJ. Christian group.

**Cancerlink** 17 Britannia Street, London WC1X 9JN (Tel: 071–833 2451). For people with cancer and their carers.

**CARE** 53 Romney Street, London SW1P 3RF (Tel: 071–233 0455).

**Carematch** 286 Camden Road, London N7 0BJ (Tel: 071–609 9966). Computer service to help find residential care for physically disabled people.

**Carers' National Association** 29 Chilworth Mews, London W2 3RG (Tel: 071–724 7776).

**Caresearch** 1 Thorpe Close, Portobello Green, London W10 5XL (Tel: 081–960 5666). Computer service for those helping people with learning difficulties.

**Cause for Concern/Causeway** Christian Concern for the Mentally Handicapped PO Box 351, Reading RG1 7AC (Tel: 0734 508781).

**Centre on Environment for the Handicapped** 35 Great Smith Street, London SW1P 3BJ (Tel: 071–222 7980).

**Church Action on Disability (CHAD)** C/o Rev John Pierce, Charisma Cottage, Drewsteignton, Exeter EX6 6RQ (Tel: 0647 21259).

**Contact A Family** 16 Strutton Ground, London SW1P 2HP (Tel: 071–222 2695/3969). For families with a child with special needs.

**Counsel and Care for the Elderly** Lower Ground Floor, Twyman House, 16 Bonny Street, London NW1 9PG (Tel: 071–485 1566).

**CRUSE** 26 Sheen Road, Richmond, Surrey TW9 1UR (Tel: 081–940 4818). Bereavement care.

**Disability Alliance** 25 Denmark Street, London WC2H 8NJ (Tel: 071–240 0806).

**Disabled Drivers' Association** Ashwellthorpe, Norwich, Norfolk NR16 1EX (Tel: 050 841 449).

**Disabled Drivers' Motor Club** Cottingham Way,

Thrapston, Northants NN1 4PL (Tel: 08012 4724).

**Disabled Living Foundation** 380–384 Harrow Road, London WL9 2HU (Tel: 071–289 6111).

**Family Fund** PO Box 50, York YO1 1UY (Tel: 0904 621115).

**Healthlines** Freepost (Rec 1828), Horsham, Sussex RH13 5ZA (Tel: 0403 210985).

**Help the Aged** 16–18 St James' Walk, London EC1R 0BE (Tel: 071–253 0253).

**Holiday Care Service** 2 Old Bank Chambers, Station Road, Horley, Surrey RH6 9HW (Tel: 0293 774535).

**Jubilee Centre** 3 Hooper Street, Cambridge CB1 2NZ (Tel: 0223 311596).

**Keep Able** 2 Capital Interchange Way, Brentford, Middlesex (081–742 2181).

**King's Fund Carers' Unit** King's Fund Centre, 126 Albert Street, London NW1 7NE (Tel: 071–267 6111).

**London Dial-A-Rider Users' Association** St Margaret's, 25 Leighton Road, London NW5 2QD (Tel: 071–482 2325).

**MENCAP** National Centre, 123 Golden Lane, London EC1Y 0RT (Tel: 071–454 0454).

**MIND (National Association for Mental Health)** 22 Harley Street, London WLN 2ED (Tel: 071–637 0741). Publications from: MIND (Publications mail), Order Service, 4th Floor, 24–32 Stephenson Way, London NW1 2HD (Tel: 071–387 9126).

**Mobility Advice and Vehicle Information Service (MAVIS)** Department of Transport, Transport and Road Research Laboratory, Crowthorne, Berkshire RG11 6AU (Tel: 0344 770456).

**Motability** 2nd Floor, Gate House, Westgate, The High, Harlow, Essex CM20 1HR (Tel: 0279 635666).

**Motor Neurone Disease Association** 61 Derngate, Northampton NN1 1VE (Tel: 0604 22269/250505).

**National Bureau for Handicapped Students** 336 Briston Road, London SW9 7AA (Tel: 071–274 0565).

**National Council for Voluntary Organisations** 26 Bedford Square, London WC1B 3HU (Tel: 071–636 8066).

**National Listening Library** 12 Lant Street, London SE1 0QH (Tel: 071–407 9417).

**National Women's Register** 245 Warwick Road, Solihull, West Midlands B92 7AH (Tel: 021 706 1101).

**Physically Handicapped and Able Bodied (PHAB)** Tavistock House North, Tavistock Square, London WC1H 9HX (Tel: 071–388 1963).

**Play Matters/National Toy Libraries' Association** 68 Churchway, London NW1 1LT (Tel: 071–387 9592).

**RADAR (Royal Association for Disability and Rehabilitation)** 25 Mortimer Street, London WIN 8AB (Tel: 071–637 5400).

**REMAP** Hazeldean, Ightam, Sevenoaks, Kent TN15 9AD (Tel: 0732 883818).

**Riding for the Disabled Association** St Clements Cottage, Ashampstead, Reading, Berks (Tel: 0635 578585).

**Spastics Society** 12 Park Crescent, London W1N 4EQ (Tel: 071–636 5020).

**Spinal Injuries Association** Newpoint, 76 St James' Lane, London N10 3DF (Tel: 081–444 2121).

**Talking Books Service (RNIB)** Mount Pleasant, Wembley, Middlesex HA0 1RR (Tel: 081–903 6666).

**Talking Newspaper Association of the United Kingdom** 90 High Street, Heathfield, East Sussex TN21 8JD (Tel: 04352 6102).

**Torch Trust for the Blind** Torch House, Hallaton, Market Harborough, Leicester (Tel: 085 889 301).

**Voluntary Council for Handicapped Children** The National Children's Bureau, 8 Wakley Street, London EC1V 7QE (Tel: 071–278 9441).

**Volunteer Information Centre** 29 Lower King's Road, Berkhampstead, Hertfordshire HP4 2AB.

# Appendix 2

## Useful Publications

*A New Deal for Carers.* Published by King's Fund and available from Bailey Distribution Ltd, Warner House, Folkestone, Kent CT19 6PH (£4.50).

*Action for Carers: A Guide to Multi-Disciplinary Support at Local Level.* Published by King's Fund and available from Bailey Distribution Ltd, Warner House, Folkestone, Kent CT19 6PH (£9.50).

*Care Attendant Schemes: Their Management and Organisation.* Published by Greater London Association for Disabled People and available from GLAD, 336 Briston Road, London SW9 7AA (50p).

*Caring for the Person with Dementia. A Guide for Families and Other Carers.* Available from Alzheimer's Disease Society (see Appendix 1 for address).

*Caring Together: Guidelines for Carers' Self-Help and Support Groups.* Available from King's Fund Centre (see Appendix 1 for address), £3.95.

*Coping with Disability.* By Peggy Jay. Published by Disabled Living Foundation (see Appendix 1 for address).

*Creating a Break: A Home Care Relief Scheme for Elderly People and Their Supporters.* Available from Age Concern (see Appendix 1 for address), £7.95.

*Dementia and Mental Illness in the Old – A Practical Guide.* By Elaine Murphy. Published by Macmillan, Papermac Health 1986.

*Dementia and the Family* (free leaflet). Barclays Bank and Mental Health Foundation, 18 Hallam Street, London W1N 6DH (Tel: 071–580 0145).

*Disability Rights Handbook.* Available from Disability Alliance (see Appendix 1 for address), £3.75.

*Disabled Persons' Railcard.* Available from local railway stations, or from British Railways Board, Central Publicity Unit, Mowbray House, Marylebone, London NW1 6JU.

*'DIY Training Course' The Local Church and Mentally Handicapped.* A Cause for Concern, PO Box 351, Reading RG1 7AC (Tel: 0734 508781).

*Door to Door. A Guide to Transport for Disabled People.* Available from Department of Transport, Freepost, South Ruislip, Middlesex HA4 0NZ.

*Enabling Voluntary Organisations to Play a Role in Supporting Carers in the Community: Some Key Issues.* Available from Care for the Carers, 143 High Street, Lewes, Sussex BN7 1XT.

*Forgetfulness in Elderly Persons.* By Tim Dowdell. Available from Age Concern, 54 Knatchbull Road, London SE5 9QY (50p).

*From Generation to Generation.* A Christian understanding of the role and care of older people. The Jubilee Centre, 3 Hooper Street, Cambridge CB1 2NZ.

*Hand in Hand (Christian Awareness Pack on Mental Handicap).* A Cause for Concern, PO Box 351, Reading RG1 7AC (Tel: 0734 508781).

*Healthlines* (At home healthcare catalogue). Freepost (Rec 1828), Horsham, W Sussex RH13 5ZA (Tel: 0403 210985).

*I Am with You – An introduction to the religious education of the mentally handicapped.* David G. Wilson, St Paul. Cause for Concern, PO Box 351, Reading RG1 7AC (Tel: 0734 508781).

*If Only I'd Known that a Year Ago.* A guide for newly disabled people, their families and friends. Published by RADAR (see Appendix 1 for address).

*It's My Duty, Isn't it? The Plight of Carers in Our Society.* By Jill Pitkeathly. Souvenir Press. Available from bookshops (£7.95).

*Keeping Fit While Caring.* Available from Family Welfare Association, 501–5 Kingsland Road, Dalston, London E8 4AU (£3.45).

*Mental Handicap & the Family* (free leaflet). Mental Health Foundation, 18 Hallam Street, London W1N 6DH.

*No Handicaps Please. We're Christian.* A Cause for Concern/Causeway, PO Box 351, Reading RG1 7AC.

*Out of Sight, Out of Mind.* A video suggesting ways in which you and your church can care for the carers. Jubilee Centre, 3 Hooper Street, Cambridge CB1 2NZ (Tel: 0223 311596).

*People in Wheelchairs – Hints for Helpers.* Red Cross Society – local branch (43p).

*Schizophrenia & the Family* (free leaflet). Barclays Bank & Mental Health Foundation, 18 Hallam Street, London W1N 6DH (Tel: 071–580 0145).

*Schizophrenia: Voices in the Dark* (CARE Series). By Mary Moate & Dr David Enoch. Published by Kingsway.

*Self-Help Groups – Getting Started, Keeping Going.* By Judy Wilson. Published by Longman (£4.95).

*Serving Carers – A Handbook for You and Your Church.* The Jubilee Centre, 3 Hooper Street, Cambridge CB1 2NZ (Tel: 0223 311596).

*Taking a Break: A Guide for People Caring at Home.* Published by King's Fund and available from Taking a Break, Newcastle-upon-Tyne X NE85 2AQ.

*The 'In Touch' Handbook.* BBC Radio 4, PO Box 7, London W3 6XJ.

*The 36-Hour Day.* By Nancy Mace and Peter Rabins. Published by Hodder & Stoughton with Age Concern. Available from bookshops (£7.50).

*Under 5s with Special Needs.* By Peter Newell and Patricia Potts. Available from Advisory Centre for Education (see Appendix 1 for address), £2.75.

*Voluntary Agencies' Directory.* From bookshops or from

Harper & Row Distributors Ltd, Estover Road, Plymouth PL6 7PZ (£7.95 in bookshops or £8.94 by post).

*Who Cares?* Available from Health Education Authority, PO Box 807, London SE99 6YE (free).

*Who's this Sitting in My Pew? Mentally Handicapped People in Church.* Faith Bowers. Triangle 1988.

# Appendix 3

## *Allowances*

### Attendance allowance (DSS – NI 205)

Available for people who need personal attention a lot of the time, such as with washing, dressing, eating and going to the toilet, or if supervision is necessary to stop the dependant hurting himself, or others. A higher rate may be claimed for people who need twenty-four-hour-a-day care. It is intended to help pay for the care required.

### Mobility allowance (DSS – NI 211)

Available for people with considerable difficulty in walking, who are aged between five and sixty-five. People in receipt of the allowance may retain it until they are seventy-five. It is paid monthly and can be used to buy a powered wheelchair, a car, pay for taxi fares, or any other purpose the disabled person wishes.

### Invalid care allowance (DSS – NI 212)

Available for people of working age who are caring for people in receipt of Attendance Allowance. The carers must spend a minimum of thirty-five hours a week looking after the disabled person. This allowance is taxable and is taken into account if other social security benefits are being claimed.

Information on the whole range of benefits is available from the Department of Social Security and the Citizens Advice Bureau.

# Appendix 4

# *DSS Booklets and Leaflets*

You can obtain these booklets and leaflets from:

Your local social security office

From some large Post Offices

By writing to: Leaflets Unit, PO Box 21, Stanmore, Middlesex HA7 1AY

By telephoning Freeline Social Security on 0800 666555.

*Attendance Allowance (NI 205)*
*Attendance Allowance: payment direct into bank or building society (NI 251)*
*Equipment and services for people with disabilities (HB 6)*
*Extra help with heating costs when it is very cold (CWP 1)*
*Going into hospital? What happens to your Social Security benefit or pension? (N 19)*
*Guide to Housing Benefit (RR 2)*
*Guide to Income Support (IS 20)*
*Guide to non-contributory benefits for disabled people (HB 5)*
*Guide to Social Fund (SB 16)*
*Guide to widow's benefit (NP 45)*
*Help with Community Charges (CCB 1)*
*Help with NHS costs (AB 11)*

*Housing benefit: help with rent and rates (RR 1)*

If you have an industrial disease: *Industrial injuries Disablement Benefit (NI 2)*

If you have pneumoconiosis or byssingosis (lung disease caused by some dusts and fibres): *Industrial Injuries Disablement Benefit (NI 3)*

*If you think your job has made you deaf (NI 207)*

*Income Support: cash help (IS 1)*

*Income Support – For people in residential care homes and nursing homes (IS 50)*

*Industrial Injuries Disablement Benefit (NI 6)*

*Invalid Care Allowance (NI 212)*

*Invalidity Benefit (NI 16A)*

*Looking after someone at home: how to protect your pension (NP 27)*

*Mobility Allowance (NI 211)*

*Mobility Allowance: payment direct into a bank or building society (NI 243)*

*Severe Disablement Allowance (NI 252)*

*Sick or Disabled? (FB 28)*

*Sick or injured through service in the armed forces? (FB 16)*

*Sickness Benefit (NI 16)*

*Social Security benefit rates (NI 196)*

*Social Security benefits – A guide for blind and partially sighted people (FB 19)*

*Statutory sick pay: check your rights (NI 244)*

*What to do after death (D 49)*

*Which benefit? (FB 2)*